LETTER HOME

The true story of the life of a British woman
married to a Kuwaiti during Saddam Hussein's
invasion of Kuwait on 2nd August 1990

BY
KAREN ALANIZI M.B.E.

To Dorothy & John with best wishes Karen Alanizi

© Copyright 2006 Karen Alanizi.
All rights reserved. No part of this publication may be reproduced, stored in a retrieval system, or transmitted, in any form or by any means, electronic, mechanical, photocopying, recording, or otherwise, without the written prior permission of the author.

Note for Librarians: A cataloguing record for this book is available from Library and Archives Canada at www.collectionscanada.ca/amicus/index-e.html
ISBN 1-4120-9954-4

Printed in Victoria, BC, Canada. Printed on paper with minimum 30% recycled fibre. Trafford's print shop runs on "green energy" from solar, wind and other environmentally-friendly power sources.

TRAFFORD
PUBLISHING™
Offices in Canada, USA, Ireland and UK

Book sales for North America and international:
Trafford Publishing, 6E–2333 Government St.,
Victoria, BC V8T 4P4 CANADA
phone 250 383 6864 (toll-free 1 888 232 4444)
fax 250 383 6804; email to orders@trafford.com

Book sales in Europe:
Trafford Publishing (UK) Limited, 9 Park End Street, 2nd Floor
Oxford, UK OX1 1HH UNITED KINGDOM
phone +44 (0)1865 722 113 (local rate 0845 230 9601)
facsimile +44 (0)1865 722 868; info.uk@trafford.com

Order online at:
trafford.com/06-1711

10 9 8 7 6 5 4 3 2 1

THANKS

To Heather whose good humour, kindness and companionship helped preserve my sanity throughout our time together during the invasion.

To Mum and Dad and Simon and Jane for their support and understanding, not just during the ordeal I put them through, but throughout my life.

To Ruth whose encouragement and excellent editing skills gave me the confidence to put my experience into words.

To Salem.....for everything.

CONTENTS

Preface	2 - 6
Map of Andalus	7
The Letter	8 - 73
The Journey Home	74 - 84
Waiting	85 - 96
Salem's Story	97 - 111
Return to Kuwait	112 - 120
Authors Note	121 - 122

PREFACE

I wrote this letter to my family during the invasion in the hope that at some time I might find a way of getting it sent back home. Because there was always the fear that it may be found I did not include anything in the letter that might give the Iraqis any excuse to cause harm to us. Therefore any mention of weapons, means of escape, resistance movements or the hiding places of westerners were not written in the original letter. I also omitted some things that I thought might increase my parent's fears for my safety if they read them! I have added these details at a later date to give a truer picture of what happened.

To give you a little bit of background, I met my husband Salem in England in 1980 and in April of 1981 we were married. I left my Mum and Dad and my brother Simon and his future wife Jane, to make a new life in Kuwait. I was welcomed with open arms by Salem's family and despite the language barrier and a severe case of culture shock I gradually adapted to my new life within the Muslim society. It must have been hard for my mother-in-law to accept the fact that her son had married not only a non-Kuwaiti that had not been previously vetted by the family, but also an infidel! I am sure that she only had Salem's best interests at heart but I soon realised that the road I had chosen to travel was not necessarily going to be a smooth one. However, the events of the summer of 1990 were to change all that.

A couple of years before the invasion occurred we had moved into our newly built house in an area called Andalus which overlooked one of the main roads that headed towards Iraq. The large house accommodated Salem's grandfather, grandmother and mother on the ground floor. On the first floor there were two separate apartments. One for Salem and myself. The other for Salem's sister Sara, her husband Jassim and my nephew Mahmoud.

Salem also has an older brother Marwan who worked for the C.I.D. Because of his position he and his family were immediately at risk when the Iraqi's invaded and he was ordered to leave the country in the early days of the invasion. This did not however prevent the Iraqis from continuing their search for him.

Salem's father, who was the head of the Al-Anizi tribe in Kuwait, did not live with us as he had re-married and had six more children. He was a small man but his presence commanded huge respect amongst both his peers and family. Even his children would sit up straight when he entered a room! I will never forget my first meeting with Salem's father shortly after my arrival in Kuwait. With Salem translating for us he said "You have left your father in England, but you have come to your father in Kuwait". I was very touched by this and I always had a soft spot for him. Salem's father, step-mother and the younger children were out of the country at the time of the invasion as were many Kuwaitis who escaped the extreme temperatures during the summer months. The eldest of Salem's step-brothers, Jamal and his pregnant wife Khawla remained in Kuwait with their young son Naif. I was to get to know them much better during the coming weeks.

When I arrived in Kuwait there were relatively

few foreigners in the country. Sami had been a college friend of Salem's in London who had married an English girl called Emily a few months before us, so I was pleased to have at least one friendly English voice to natter with! Emily had gone back to England to visit her parents, leaving Sami in Kuwait that fateful summer. Through Emily I met Heather who had been a nurse in Bristol when she met her Kuwaiti husband Yousef. They married and moved to Kuwait where, luckily for me, she moved into her mother-in-laws house close by. Heather and Yousef had a boat and we used to spend many enjoyable Fridays going out to the coral reefs at Kubar Island. We were not at all happy that Saddam Hussein had chosen to invade us just before the weekend and messed up our plans for a day out at sea!

Having discovered that being a lady of leisure was not all it was cracked up to be, and to prevent myself from going insane with boredom, I managed to become gainfully employed. At the time of the invasion I worked for a furnishing company that sold and rented furniture, mostly to the ex-patriot community. Located in Andalus, it was owned by two English couples Sally and Ken, and Paula and Geoff. The other English member of staff and a good friend was the lovely Pat who lived with her husband Alex in nearby Grenata.

On the 1st August 1990 I was chatting to Heather on the phone when she said how bored she was feeling and that she really wished something exciting would happen.

Be careful what you wish for………..

Letter Home

MAP OF ANDALUS AREA

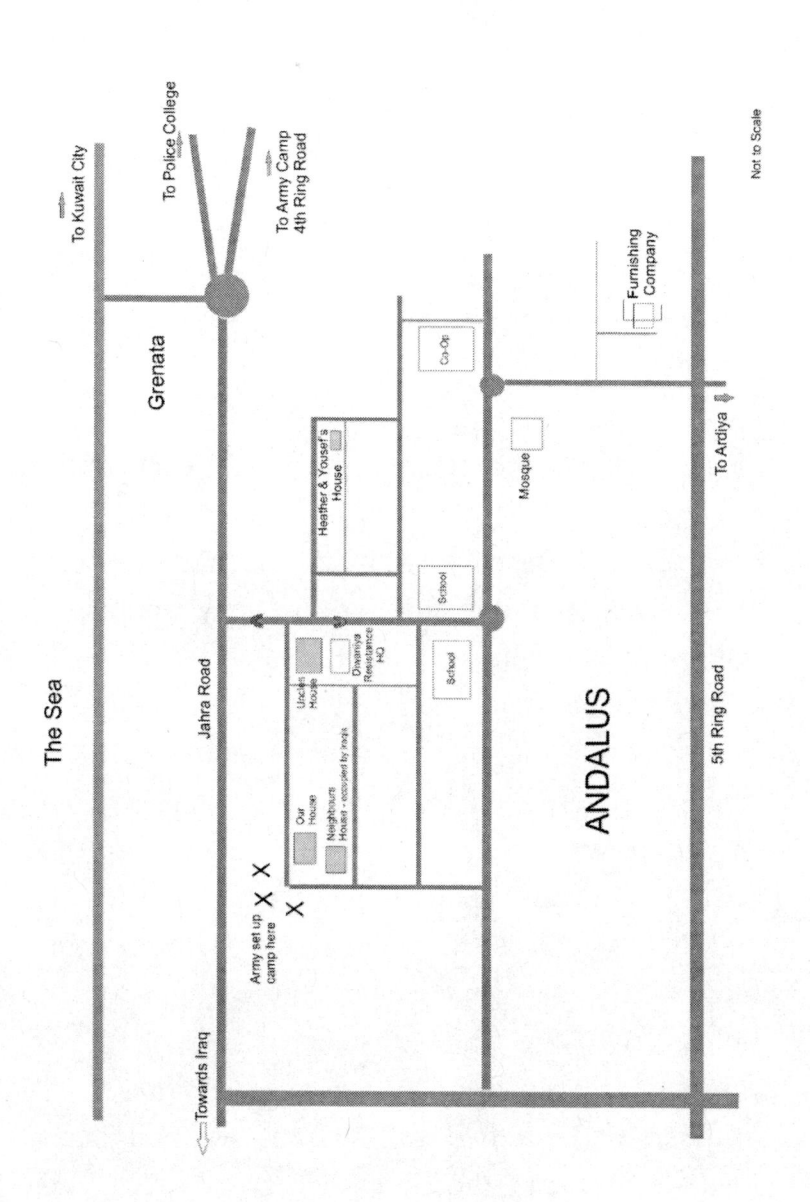

THE LETTER

Dear Mum & Dad (please pass on to Simon and Jane),

Today is Sunday 5th August 1990, Day 4 of the Iraqi invasion. I'll start writing now and keep going until I'm able to post this to you, let's hope it doesn't turn into a book! I was woken up on Thursday morning by a booming sound, which we later discovered was gunfire. It sounded like someone was moving furniture around in the room downstairs. I thought it was a bit odd but was half asleep, so took no notice. At 6am the intercom buzzer went, Salem wanted to ignore it but I told him there'd been a lot of noise downstairs and thought we should answer it. Marwan had phoned to say that we had been invaded and that the Iraqi's were already in the

City. *He asked Salem if he had any weapons in the house that we could use to arm ourselves if necessary. After talking with the rest of the family, Salem told me to gather together our passports and any other important documents and pack them in a small bag in case we had to make a hasty escape. The uncertainty of what was happening and what might happen next was very unnerving.* I didn't quite believe it until Pat phoned to say that Alex's colleague had been shot at on the way to work and that all the roads into Kuwait were blocked. That's when I phoned you. I was very fortunate to get through by all accounts. It didn't seem real until all the tanks and armoured cars started pouring down the road in front of us around nine o'clock. They kept coming for a good two hours and have drifted in intermittently ever since. The phone never stopped ringing with rumours flying all over the place.

Emily called from England asking me if I knew that we'd been invaded! She had spoken to Sami who was at the factory in the industrial area and he had no idea what was going on!

Paula called to tell me not to go to work!

They set up camp right outside our building

and installed six big anti-aircraft guns pointing at the house and twelve more at the side. Two plumes of smoke rose from the army camps and one from the city. The sound of gun fire was very loud. Salem decided it would be better to move down to his Uncle's house so we could all be together. Unfortunately there is still a bit of a family feud going on so the atmosphere wasn't too wonderful. Gunfire went on until about 9pm and then it went quiet until the early morning when it started all over again.

We sat glued to the World Service every hour to try and find out what was going on. Soldiers are everywhere but don't bother anyone. They just use the water from the garden taps, although we have seen some soldiers driving civilian cars and believe they've looted some of the shops for food. On Friday afternoon a convoy of Iraqi civilians arrived, headed by a Mercedes and a radio car with some army officers. They stopped mid-way between our house and Uncles house where they got water. About five hundred people in all. They hung around for about an hour then all of a sudden turned around and went back towards Iraq.

Salem and I came back to the house on our

own to collect some things, have a shower and a proper cup of coffee, bliss! While we were there an army water tank broke down outside the house. The men got fed up with pushing it and started poking around Granddad's garden. When they started climbing on the wall to look over the top, Salem decided we should leave and come back later, in numbers. We'd heard rumours that soldiers had been into private houses taking gold and valuables, but nothing like that had happened in Andalus yet.

By now the fires had stopped burning and there was only the occasional gun shots going off. We had been keeping in touch all the time with Heather and Yousef but the phone lines to Cathy and Alec, who live in Abu Halifa on the other side of the country, by now, were down.

By Saturday Kuwaiti's were going out in their cars to see what was going on, get food and petrol. We went over to see Heather and Yousef and all of us, including Yousef's mother, went out for a drive to have a look. Heather and I wore abayas*! What a sight! There were lots of Iraqi army checks everywhere. We went past the army

*The full length black cloak worn over the clothes by Muslim women.

camp. My God, what destruction, burnt out army tanks, great big holes in walls, hundreds of burnt cars. Durrah Complex in Reggae must have been used by the Iraqis to fire on the National Guard, which is opposite, as it had two great big holes in its side. The Emir's palace was surrounded by burnt out tanks and cars and the British Embassy and Kuwait Towers had their windows shot out. *At the entrance to the Emirs palace was an abandoned car with a bisht* laying over the back window. We later discovered that this belonged to Sheikh Fahad, the Crown Prince's brother, who was killed in his attempt to prevent the Iraqi's entering the royal palace.* There was a distinct smell around the palace, one I hadn't smelt before….the smell of death. The amount of traffic on the roads was amazing. Of all the checks we went through only once were we stopped and had the boot and glove compartment searched. We came back past the Bayan palace, which had all the guard posts blasted out. Everywhere there were deserted cars, most of which had been looted. All along the sea front there are tanks and missile launchers, about thirty or so opposite our street.

*A n outer robe worn by men over their clothes.

We were happy to hear on the news that the troops were going to leave, but today we've seen no evidence to support their claims. At one point all the big guns outside started to pack up but they only moved position and still have us surrounded!!

Today we've been back at home most of the day, mainly due to a big argument between Salem's Mum and Aunt! It's nice to be at home again although we did have a panic earlier. Salem went down to Uncle's house and while he was there we heard heavy machine gun fire. I phoned his Uncles house and they said that Salem had left for home. When he didn't turn up and the firing went on we got really worried. *The machine gun fire was very loud and sounded really close. Presumably there were Kuwaitis putting up some kind of resistance near by.* I gathered all the family together in a corridor downstairs where we were away from any windows; in case of any stray bullets. Sara sat with the Koran, reading aloud as Salem's mother started to panic. Granddad, who is quite deaf without his hearing aid, couldn't understand what all the fuss was about as he couldn't hear the gun fire. It took a lot of pleading to stop him from going outside!* Then

Salem phoned to say that he had been at the diwaniya* but had returned to his Uncle's house when the gunfire started. As soon as it quietened down he came home, safe and sound. The rumour was that Saddam Hussein had been killed and that now the Iraqi soldiers were fighting each other! Nothing on the news, so I don't know how true it is. Now everything's quiet it's boring again.

Andalus has started a kind of Neighbourhood Watch. *Guns have been distributed to all the houses. All Kuwaiti's have to do two years National Service so are familiar with weapons and how to use them.* They've got the clinic operating and the co-op is open and rationing food out. If you don't have any money you can sign for it and pay when you can. They also have guards to prevent looting of the shops.

Monday – Day 5

All quiet on the western front! We're just sitting and waiting now to see what's going to happen next. The World Service seems to think Bush is going to get us out of this. If it's by economic sanctions it could take a long time. Military intervention would be quicker but could

*A gathering place where men meet.

turn a bit nasty for us. We can only wait and see, and hope for the best. The soldiers outside the house are digging trenches and obviously aren't moving out. Our wonderful new Iraqi government, which keeps making television announcements, showed videos last night of troops supposedly leaving Kuwait. It was filmed in Sulaibikhat but we didn't see anything like the numbers filmed go past our house. No-one believes them and take no notice of anything they say. They haven't even shown a picture of any of our new supposed leaders!

Salem has just come back from getting sacks of rice and flour, chicken and meat to keep us going, as whatever happens there's going to be a food shortage. The soldiers have been washing themselves at the water tap outside the house behind us and Salem told them off for showing their bodies in front of houses where there were women. They dutifully went to the tap around the corner where no-one could see them! Salem's grandfather came to tell me in his wonderful English "You no look, soldier's trousers down"! *Salem's grandfather learnt his English when as a younger man he worked for the British Army when they were based in Kuwait the last time we had* *some trouble with the Iraqis. His English sentences are often filled with expletives, which he thinks are used in normal conversation! This caused some amusement when meeting my parents for the first time, having asked them how they were and then replying that they were fine, he said "Just the f***ing job!". He also speaks fluent Farsi and Hindi from his days aboard the ships that used to sail to Iran and India to trade in spices, dates and water.*

Tuesday – Day 6

Last night Salem and Yousef went to the mosque, where all the men are now meeting that want to help with the Neighbourhood Watch cum Community Aid project. They went around all the diwaniyas telling everyone what was going on and enlisting help. The problem now is not the soldiers but the Indians and Palestinians who are stealing. Quite what they are going to do with their booty I don't know. We heard some interesting gossip too. Seven soldiers went to a house in Andalus asking for water. The owner obliged and started talking to them. He asked them why they were doing this to Kuwait after we had helped them in their war against Iran. Their reply was that they had come because we had asked them to help us against our evil rulers! The man brought them a short wave radio so they could hear what the rest of the world was saying. Having discovered the truth they then asked for dishdashas* and left their uniforms and guns behind, heading for the border!

The co-op, which is now controlled by the Neighbourhood Watch, was approached by two soldiers who wanted food. The Kuwaitis told them no, they had their own army rations and if they took anything they would inform their commander. At this they started begging them not to, as their commander would execute them if they were found to be disobeying orders.

We had a panic last night around 2am. Suddenly orders were being given over a loud hailer and the anti-aircraft guns were going up, ready for action. We shot downstairs, but after a while it seemed that it was only a practice. Panic over.

Our new imposed government has announced that everyone can return to work today. Of course, no-one has. Everything they say is ignored and disbelieved by everyone. I don't know who they're trying to kid!

*A floor length garment worn by Arab men.

Pat phoned this afternoon. They had a bit of a rough time with the troops in Grenata so moved to the Regency Palace Hotel as they felt safer in numbers. *Unlike us they live in a more secluded area and the soldiers can be more aggressive to get what they want without fear of reprisal from their superiors who can't see what they're up to.* They are hoping to get out when they can and will phone you to let you know I'm OK. I also spoke to Paula who has gone to stay with friends in Jabriya. She wanted to know where the company insurance papers were! I don't think war is covered.

Thursday – Day 8

On Tuesday night at midnight all the Kuwaitis were up on their roofs with the lights on cheering. There is a lot of resistance among the Kuwaitis and all sorts of things are going on which I won't explain now, but it's keeping everyone's spirits up. *Apart from organizing the distribution of weapons to every household the resistance is involved in many efforts to disrupt Iraqi operations. These include regular remote controlled explosions in places where the soldiers gather. A Kuwaiti girl filled her car with explosives and drove it into an Iraqi camp, giving up her own life for the cause.*

Every night we now sleep in Uncle's basement, just in case. *I sleep with a loaded handgun under my pillow, not that I would know how to use it should I need to!* Everyone feels that military intervention is inevitable at some point. I just wish they'd get on with it!

I spent the whole of yesterday at Heather's – we're keeping each other sane! I'm so glad we met before all this happened and what would we do without the World Service to let us know what's going on in the rest of the world? Of all the news yesterday we liked the bit that said an American newspaper headline was "Up Yours"! Yesterday, Saddam (or Sod'em as the Americans say) told us that we are now Iraq. He's a nutcase. No-one will take any notice of him, least of all the Kuwaitis here.

Friday Day 9

Well this is getting very boring. Apart from occasional gun fire, nothing much is happening. Heather and I have a marathon game of monopoly going on.

The men have been talking to the soldiers. The Iraqi's have no idea what they're up against. I feel sorry for most of them; they don't like what's going on either. They get paid fifteen Iraqi Dinars a month (about three pounds sterling). It's officially twenty two Dinars but they take off money for "The Party" and money for a new stadium which is being built! Salem offered one of them five hundred Kuwaiti Dinars* for his machine gun but he said that if he went back without it he would probably be shot.

*One Kuwait Dinar equals around two pounds sterling.

Saturday – Day 10

Well, everyone agrees that Saddam Hussein has gone completely mad! The only TV we get now is propaganda – pictures of Saddam Hussein with "All the Arab world is with Iraq" written underneath and so-called religious men condemning the West and the Kuwaiti ruling family (I'm sure that's not allowed in the Koran), and crowds of people cheering for "Victory Day"!! The soldiers say that they just drag people onto the streets to support Saddam and if they don't do what they're asked their families are threatened.

We heard on the radio that a Help Line has been set up in the Bristol area. I hope it's useful to you. It's awful not being able to let you know that we're alright.

We were woken at 6am this morning. A soldier was inside the gates of Uncle's house. **From our** *basement sleeping place I watched through the narrow windows at ceiling height as this pair of khaki covered legs walked past, nearing the front entrance. My hand moved to the hand gun under my pillow and I shook Salem awake.* The soldier was unarmed but none-the-less didn't get the chance to say what he wanted before Salem's Uncle kicked him out. I must say Salem's uncle has been very kind to us. We all turn up every evening and are fed before we go to sleep and get breakfast every morning before we leave. What with all the other relatives and children there must be about twenty of us here. Thank goodness there are also five maids and a couple of houseboys to cope with this lot. It does feel a lot safer in numbers and I know Salem is more relaxed with a few able men around. Everyone's mood swings with each piece of news we get, but most of the time everyone is cheerful. We have electricity and water and plenty of food, so can't complain. It's just the waiting that gets to everyone, especially when your friend has hotels on Park Lane and Mayfair!!

It's very hot today, the Americans and Brits arriving in Saudi are going to find it tough.

Sunday – Day 11

Well the good news this morning is that all the anti-aircraft guns around our house are moving out. What a relief. I don't think there are any troops in Andalus anymore. Yesterday around fifty tanks, thirty missile launchers and fifty armoured cars came out of the city, but then went across the back of the house out towards the 7th Ring Road. Probably down to the Saudi border. It looks as if the soldiers in Andalus are headed that way too.

I decided to hide our jewellery and watches somewhere safe so packed them all together and after much deliberation hid them up in the air conditioning duct in the sitting room. All around the country similar hiding places are being found for much larger stashes than ours. Thousands of Dinars worth of gold and jewellery is being buried in gardens. I spent one afternoon stitching wads of Dinar notes into pillows and cushions. I never thought I'd be doing something like that, I felt like a bank robber!

Well another bit of excitement. *Salem had gone up to Uncles house leaving me with the job of making an ankle holster for his gun. Before he left I asked him to take the bullets out, just in case I accidentally shot myself in the process! I had the gun, bullets and some fabric laid out on the ironing board in our spare room, which looks out over the front of the house.* The door bell rang and outside was a white Mercedes with some military officers in it and two trucks with machine guns on top carrying a load of red-capped soldiers. *I immediately called Salem and asked him if I should hide the gun or get ready to use it, and if the latter how did I get the damn bullets back in the gun!* He told me to hide it and suggested putting it in the toilet cistern. *Having put the phone down I then quickly pondered whether a gun would go rusty if it was put directly into water and thought I'd better seal it in a plastic bag! Fortunately before I got around to hiding it they moved on!* They asked whose house it was and how many people lived here. Granddad told them that there are far more here than there actually are, and so they moved on to the next house, which unfortunately is unoccupied. They all had a good look around, left one man there and moved on. I hope they're not going to use it as their new headquarters. They left the other house (near Heather's) two days ago.

We've just heard that the British Embassy is able to telex out names of people who are OK. I'm still trying to get through to them so that they can let you know we're alright.

Apparently at Alghanim, the General Motors Agents, just down the 4th Ring Road, they have absolutely destroyed everything. All the cars have been broken into and then burnt.

Monday – Day 12

Well fortunately the soldiers next door moved away from the house before nightfall.

Jamal has come to stay with us for a while. He was working in the military hospital when this started so was held there to help with all the casualties. He said that there were far more Iraqis than Kuwaitis and that the Iraqis were very young and scared. Some of them were wearing flip flops instead of army boots and their rations consisted of one pita bread filled with salad greens. Jamal said that they only managed to get away from the hospital the day before yesterday.

I spoke to the British Embassy warden who said they were trying to get messages back to England. I hope they succeed. Abdullah from work also phoned, all the staff are OK, but can you believe that on the second day, the Kuwaiti Partner asked him to come and move furniture from one of his houses to the other!

I forgot to mention that we were informed by the new unwanted government that everyone who failed to turn up for work the day before yesterday was fired! Needless to say, all of Kuwait was fired!

Tuesday – Day 13

Something very strange is going on in the house behind us. Apparently the soldiers didn't go after all but are making themselves as inconspicuous as possible. Salem and Yousef went round there yesterday, thinking that the soldiers had left, to see if the Indian houseboy was OK after the Iraqis visit. They were surprised to be met by a soldier with a machine gun who said that there was no-one there and that they shouldn't go near the house again. Later they brought a pick-up truck right inside the gates, checked through binoculars and then brought something into the house. The mirrored windows are fantastic for watching what's going on without being seen. I'd love to know what they're up to.

There appears to be very little troop movement now the attention has been drawn to the Saudi border. There are a lot of empty trucks coming in and full ones going out. Rich pickings! Salmiya high street has apparently been completely looted. All those lovely diamond watches have gone to somebody!

All imported goods are now in short supply. No sliced bread or fresh fruit. Salem brought me loads of chocolate yesterday, and shampoo and toothpaste, which is available now but will soon not be. We have enough rice, lentils and flour to last several years I think!

Heather came over yesterday for the first time, as Yousef wasn't too keen on her coming with all the troops and guns around before. She was so excited by the view we have here, as they can't see anything where they are.

Wednesday – Day 14

Jamals wife and little boy, Naif, came to stay yesterday. His wife Khawla is very nice and speaks excellent English. There was quite a bit of machine gun fire last night but we couldn't work out where it was coming from.

This morning there were some comings and goings at our neighbours. This time four Mercedes with officers in and three car loads of commandos, who surrounded the building before one of the Mercedes went in through the gates so the V.I.P. could get out. I'd love to know what's going on.

The British Embassy phoned today. Apparently

all British diplomats will be leaving with an armed escort for Baghdad tomorrow! If I wanted to go I would have to provide my own transport, food, petrol etc! It sounds like out of the frying pan into the fire to me. The diplomats apparently have no choice. The warden apologized but said that he was obliged to give me the opportunity to go if I wanted to. He is staying here!

Thursday – Day 15

Some troops have moved back and camped on the other side of the 4th Ring Road. Not many, most of them went over by the sea. Jamal, Khawla and Naif went home today but will be coming back again if there are any more fights at their mother's house! The situation doesn't bring out the best in Kuwaiti women. Jamal and family are very nice but it is good to have the flat back to ourselves again. Although there's always someone going in and out because we have such a good view!

Friday – Day 16

A bit of excitement yesterday with this announcement asking all Brits and Americans to report to the Hyatt Regency or face "unspecified difficulties"! Of course the majority of people didn't go – we phoned the Embassy warden and he said that "some bloody idiots had actually gone", but had been turned away. He said he didn't bother to phone us as he knew we wouldn't have much difficulty in hiding if necessary as we lived with Kuwaiti families. He also assured us that all lists of names will be destroyed. However, today it seems that the Iraqi's don't know anything about it!

I decided to move the jewellery stash from the air-conditioning duct as this is apparently the first place that the Iraqi's search. It is now in the cavity in the front of the loudspeaker unit!

The Iraqi's are taking everything they can out of Kuwait while they're able. Yesterday all the Kuwaiti tanks went out and lorry loads of furniture too. Containers from the port are also pouring out. It's sickening. We've even seen truck loads of Post Office boxes and traffic lights heading back to Iraq!

As electronics are one of the first things to be looted I moved the jewellery stash again and buried it in the earth of one of our unhealthy looking pot plants! Passes the time!

A lot of families are leaving for Saudi, but if Iraq makes a move in that direction I don't think it will be very safe there either.

Saturday – Day 17

Well we're officially hostages today. This could escalate things a bit. Last night there was very heavy gun fire over by the sea and one of the anti-aircraft guns was also fired. But it quietened down later. Pat said that the soldiers came to check the hotel register yesterday. The hotel has satellite TV and she had seen some people we know, who had escaped through the desert yesterday, being interviewed on the news. Among them, Sally and Ken's son, the wife of the KAC pilot who was hijacked and her daughters, and two other English couples who I think you have met before. I bet Sally and Ken are relieved! Paula decided not to go with them.

Some of the passengers and crew of the British Airways flight that had landed in Kuwait shortly before the hostilities began are also living at the Hyatt Regency.

More tanks, troops etc. have been pouring in since yesterday afternoon.

Salem's Dad was seen on Saudi TV last night explaining his situation and giving Saddam Hussein a mouthful! Unfortunately we can't get any of the other Gulf channels in Andalus, but strangely Iraq TV, which has also been transmitting on Kuwait channels has not been on at all today, which has started rumours of revolution in Iraq again. Can you believe that yesterday on Iraq TV they showed a newspaper which printed a letter that Saddam Hussein had written to the Prophet Mohamed! Nutcase!

Sunday – Day 18

Happy Birthday Simon! I have got you a card but couldn't manage to post it!

Iraq TV is back on again, false alarm! I haven't had my daily phone call from Pat today. I'm afraid that they might have been carted off to Baghdad.

Salem's grandfather had a car accident this morning. He's OK thank goodness. Some idiot went through a red light and smashed into the side of him. The car doesn't look too good.

When the Iraqi's search houses they are looking for military men and police and if they find any uniforms immediately arrest the men of the house. What they don't realize is that as all men do National Service for one month every year, practically every household has military uniforms in it. We decided to dispose of Salem's uniforms today and packed them into a rubbish bag and set fire to them in the garden.

Loads of tanks have been coming in again this

afternoon. It seems never ending. The resistance is still strong here however and it seems the Iraqis will sell anything. There is even a price list going around! Kuwaitis are buying tanks and then blowing them up! You can also get relatives released who have been taken prisoner for the right amount of money. A machine gun costs only KD. 10!

Monday – Day 19

Well we are surrounded again, we have a camp right beside the house, but at least the anti-aircraft guns are half the size of the last ones!

Khawla and Naif are back and they brought with them a video of the news from Saudi Arabia, Qatar and the Kuwait transmission from Saudi Arabia. It's the first time I've seen Salem's Mum smile for ages. When they showed all the American planes and ships arriving she was cheering and clapping! As you can imagine she's been all doom and gloom since this started, not to mention that every time there is a gun shot (which is quite often) she rushes upstairs with her toothbrush saying that we must go back to uncle's basement! At least she's talking to me!

I spoke to Paula yesterday – she sounded very down in the dumps – upset about Pat and Alex being moved from the Hyatt Regency and wishing she hadn't been too scared to escape with the others. *She had already had one attempt going out through the desert which was aborted after they got shot at.*

Just heard from one of the American wardens that the people taken from the Hotels are all being held in one of those huge villas on the Gulf Road and that they are all well and safe. We also heard that some American Arabs with British wives who went shopping yesterday and were all done up in abayas were stopped. The wives were taken but the men, who had American passports but were originally Palestinian, were allowed to leave. So I am now housebound, and not even allowed to go down to Heathers in my abaya, as we have troops around us again.

Tuesday – Day 20

Well I did manage to get over to Heather's yesterday, the scouts were sent out to make sure there were no checks on the route and Yousef's Mum had dug out some burgas* and all the Bedouin gear for both of us. What a sight. I never

---

*A black veil with two slits for the eyes worn over the face by Muslim women.

realized how difficult it is to wear. The abaya keeps slipping off the back of my head and the centre piece of the burga, which is supposed to go down the middle of the nose, keeps sliding over one eye! It certainly gave everyone a laugh when we got home! Yousef's mother is totally the opposite of Salem's Mum. She would quite happily go out there and beat the Iraqi's senseless with a broomstick if it would help, she's not at all afraid. Salem's Mum makes me whisper when she sees an army crane half a mile away and constantly declares that we are all going to die from chemical weapons and that our skin will melt from our bones!

Salem and Yousef drove down the Gulf Road yesterday and were surprised to find that all the tanks had gone. Only six tanks left along the whole length of the Gulf Road. Very strange! I wonder what they're up to now.

Yesterday the sons of the house behind us came home which caused a bit of a stir among the commandos living there. They told them to phone at 4pm and they'd let them know if they could move back in. Apparently they said they would leave in one week's time! So we still have our unwelcome visitors next door!

Thursday – Day 22

Yesterday morning Cathy and Alec phoned. They were two of the eight people taken from their homes by twelve soldiers last night at 10pm. They sounded in good spirits and said that they had been treated well. They were being kept at the Meridien Hotel in Kuwait City. It was great to know that they were OK but we know that the phones are being monitored and Salem was particularly worried that as there were only eight of them at the Hotel it would be easy for them to track down anyone that they might speak to, either by phone number records or by forcing Cathy and Alec to tell them our address. *Cathy and Alec had also asked about Salem's brother Marwan who is in the C.I.D. and was actively being searched for by the Iraqi's. He had been ordered to leave with his family on the third day of the invasion, but the search for him had already spread to his father's house. It was only a matter of time before it reached us in Andalus.* So we are now in hiding at Heather and Yousef's, just in case! We're banned from using the phone too! Yousef has attached an answering machine so that we know who calls, even if we can't speak to them!

Yesterday night we heard first hand that marines had been spotted at Shuaiba Refinery. Could this be true?

Friday – Day 23

Well we thought that Saddam Hussein's discussion with the British Hostages with that poor boy sitting beside him was quite revolting and were glad to hear that Britain's official reaction was the same!

There are now army checks inside Andalus, so it doesn't look as if I'll be going home in the near future.

It will be interesting to see what happens today as the diplomats lose their diplomatic immunity and the Embassies are forced to close. If the Iraqis raid the Embassies then I guess that is officially attacking that Embassy's country. Perhaps this will give them the excuse to finally attack Iraq. We're all fed up with waiting!

There's not so much news to give you now we've moved away from the roadside view!

Saturday – Day 24

Heather and I have decided to write a book, on the lighter side of the invasion! Heather had already decided to do a course on writing and has two huge volumes which the college sent her on how to do it properly, so yesterday we started jotting down our ideas, hopefully we'll be able to make some sense out of them! At least it will keep us amused while we're confined to the house! I was hoping to get home sometime yesterday but there are still road checks inside Andalus and on top of the school there are soldiers with bazookas.

Sunday – Day 25

Well I think one of the bazookas went off last night. It was incredibly loud with a lot of machine gun fire following it. We also heard the news today that those found harbouring foreigners will be hung, which is not very nice. Heather and I have decided that if there is anything to suggest that this is more than an idle threat we will go into hiding somewhere on our own so that we're no risk to anyone else.

Cathy phoned this morning to say that they were being moved from the Hotel today, but they don't know where.

A little while ago a bomb went off at the roundabout. The resistance is attacking at all times of the day and night now. It must keep the Iraqis on their toes! *There is a junction which you can see from our house, on the way to*

Sulaibikhat, where there is a small restaurant that is used by the truck drivers that are looting. The resistance blow it up every couple of weeks. On one occasion a member of the resistance came to the house looking for Salem to warn us that in ten minutes there would be a huge explosion at the restaurant and that we should take cover. We moved away from the windows and waited anxiously. Sure enough moments later there was a massive bang and black smoke billowed up from the restaurant.

Iraqi propaganda TV is sometimes quite amusing! Yesterday they gave out the address of Bush and Thatcher and told all the Iraqis to write to them in protest! Then they showed a video of a British couple from Kuwait getting married in a Hotel in Baghdad, courtesy of the generous Iraqis of course!

Monday – Day 26

Happy Birthday Mum! We're thinking of you, even if we can't have our usual chat on the phone! Nothing exciting to report yet. We all seem to be sleeping later in the morning and staying up later at night. We've turned into Salems! Yousef has a computer which is well equipped with games, so while he and Salem are not at the diwaniya gathering news they're usually learning how to land planes, shoot down Iraqi fighters and even do hospital operations! As far as the operations went they managed to kill the patient before they even got to operate!

Tuesday – Day 27

Salem and Yousef got up early this morning to go and register at the co-op. In a couple of day's time, six months supply of food will be delivered to the house. Someone has been getting things organised! They have started searching the houses in some areas looking for foreigners and weapons. Looks like the burga and abaya are going to be ready in case of emergencies again!

Yesterday I attacked Heather's hair with the curling tongs. Yousef's Mum now calls her Barbie!

Wednesday – Day 28

Yesterday they started searching the houses one by one. *This is the most scared I've been since this began. If the Iraqi's discover that Heather and I are westerners they will execute our husbands. We sat in Heather's living room wearing headscarves and abayas...waiting. Heather's Arabic is very good as she chats to her mother-in-law every day. I on the other hand could never pass as a Kuwaiti. With my heart pounding we attempt to recite the Lords Prayer and shamefully can't remember all the words. Despite this, God must have realized our hearts were in it, as he looked after us that day.* They searched Salem's Uncle's house and our house but didn't get around to Heather and Yousef's and haven't been searching today either, so we were very lucky.

The British Embassy warden phoned to check if we wanted to leave, just in case Saddam Hussein's latest offer to release women and children is true. Saddam seems to change his mind every five minutes! The warden and his wife are staying in Kuwait whatever happens. They've been here twelve years and have lots of pets. I know that you'd want me to come home if I get the chance but I can't leave Salem here, not being able to get in touch with him and know he's alright. I love Kuwait, and feel sure that one way or another we'll get it back, although it will never be the same again. I'd feel as if I was running away if I left now. If it's true that women and children will not be considered hostages things should ease up a bit and Heather and I won't have to sneak around anymore!

Some foods are in short supply but we're certainly not suffering for it. Food that is available is free. Last night a group of young lads came round on a truck delivering bread to all the houses. They also collect and burn the rubbish. Salem's grandmother says that it is like the old days when people cared about each other and not about who had the latest model Mercedes! There certainly is a great community spirit.

Hopefully I might be able to get this letter out with someone who is leaving. I'll give you Heather's Mums telephone number so that you can keep in touch should either one of us be able to get messages out, so you'll know we're both OK. I don't know whether Cathy will leave Alec behind or not, but as she's already one of Saddam Hussein's "guests" she's likely to get out early. Her Mum's phone number is xxxx, although by the time we spoke to them here we couldn't say much as the phones were monitored. *Even though we didn't really believe that we were being listened in to, it was rather strange that when I was talking to Heather about the Iraqi soldier whose body was hanging from a crane (apparently hung by his commander when he was caught looting) and we said that it should be Saddam Hussein hanging from that crane, the phone line was instantly cut off and remained dead for around 10 minutes!*

Thursday – Day 29

Our days seem to consist of sleeping, eating and listening to the news! Sometimes there's some funny propaganda on TV which gives us a good laugh and of course Saddam Hussein's interviews more recently. The last programme on TV every night is usually an English film, but never less than twenty years old! The only up to date thing they show us is "Beauty and the Beast", exactly the same episodes as we recently watched on Kuwait TV!

Friday – Day 30

A month is almost up and Saddam Hussein has declared that Kuwait is now officially the 19th Province of Iraq. In some ways it's gone so quickly in others it's gone so slowly. Most of the last month has been spent listening to the radio and looking out of the window! It's been quite quiet around Andalus the last couple of days but apparently last night there was a lot of fighting in Kuwait City. Yesterday the rumour was that the marines had been spotted in Basra! It's getting to be quite a joke as to where they'll be seen next! It conjures up visions of them only being visible to Kuwaitis and invisible to the Iraqis! However unbelievable some of these rumours are it still manages to raise people's spirits. I'm surprised someone hasn't seen Rambo yet! He's sure to sort everything out!

Saturday – Day 31

Yesterday Yousef cut Salem's hair for him – with a beard trimmer! He looks like he's just come out of the army again! It was so long before; he could have had a ponytail! Trendy, I thought! I wonder when I'll get my hair done. At least this is one way of growing it long and having a good excuse for it looking a mess! Carla, who was going to do it for me is married to an Iraqi. I wonder what's happened to her.

There's nothing much else to report today – so far!

Sunday – Day 32

Last night was fantastic! The word had got around again that everyone should go up on their roofs at midnight and shout "Allah Akbar" (God is Great). At about five to twelve you could hear it start way off in the distance and then get louder and louder as everyone joined in, children, women, everyone shouting at the tops of their voices. Machine guns were going off and the tracer bullets lit up the sky like fireworks. The resistance had rigged up all sorts of things that sounded like cannon going off. An Iraqi camp nearby just up and fled back towards Iraq. They must have wondered what on earth was going on, especially as only a few days ago all the houses were searched for weapons and now guns were going off all over the place! It really got everyone in a great mood, although a stray bullet did hit the water tank on the roof of Sara's apartment, back at the house.

Today everyone is on strike! The second of September, one month since the invasion. Nothing is open and no-one is leaving their houses. That should make the Iraqi's suspicious of what's going on too!

We've heard on the radio that the first lot of hostages have arrived home and believe that Pat was among them. She has your and Heather's Mum's phone numbers, so hopefully she'll phone you soon.

We heard that both Safeway and Sultan Centre supermarkets have been burnt down and that the Iraqis have raided all the Sheikhs houses and taken everything, including the Arab horses. Nothing is left – what they can't take they've burnt down. As far as I know the furniture showroom is more or less intact, being off the beaten track. I'm fed up with not being able to go to work. Heather and I actually went outside yesterday to wash down the courtyard, all done up in our headscarves! Stupid things kept falling off, and they're so hot!

Monday – Day 33

Yesterday there was a message on the answering machine from a friend of Heather's called Kathryn – she said she would be leaving in the next two days on an emergency flight as she was pregnant and would pass on any messages to our parents. We got all excited and then when Heather phoned her today it had all fallen through as her British warden had been taken from his home. Apparently a lot of people have been taken but as there is no contact with the Embassies anymore no-one knows about it.

The soldiers are just waiting for people to run out of food and as soon as they put their heads out of the door they are taken. *We hear of people hiding for hours on end concealed in air conditioning ducts and inside half empty water* tanks on the roofs of houses, when the Iraqis are searching their area. Kuwaitis, who know of westerners in hiding, are risking their own lives to get food and supplies to them.

None of the Iraqi radio stations are on the air today. This has sparked off all sorts of rumours! We are waiting to see if the World Service correspondent in Iraq is allowed to speak today.

Tuesday – Day 34

Well the convoy of British women and children left today at 6am from Sultan Centre. It looks as if it's mostly those women with children. A lot of women have chosen to stay with their husbands. Amongst those who have left is Heather's friend Kathryn, who will phone you, if and when she gets back to England, to reassure you that we're all OK. Heather say's she's a bit "doom and gloom", so I hope she doesn't make out that it's worse than it is. We will be following their progress on the World Service.

Wednesday – Day 35

I spent yesterday evening and this morning making gas masks! Like surgical masks with a pocket in the front which will be filled with crushed charcoal, which is supposed to absorb any toxic things in the air. I wouldn't be surprised if Salem's Mum makes us wear them all the time! Yousef's Mum is going to do the charcoal filling this evening and has been washing the dust out of the charcoal and drying it all day. No doubt we will end up making loads of them once the word gets round! It's so nice to be busy doing something useful for a change. These gas masks should work with the nerve gas, but for mustard gas we have to get under the shower as well! If war does break out we shall probably be walking around dripping wet most of the time! Things have been quite quiet the last few days and now the threat to women and children is no longer on we will probably go back home soon and return to our daily visits to each other houses. Heather and Yousef are such a nice couple and we have had a few laughs through all of this. I do hope you get to speak to Heather's parents – hopefully they'll be happy to see Yousef when all this is over. It's taken them three years to realize that it was not just a passing fancy! I'm sure if they'd met him they would have changed their minds.

Happy Birthday Dad!

Thursday – Day 36

We've heard that the Kuwaiti, Saudi, Egyptian

and American troops have moved over the Saudi border and are now in Wafra! Let's hope they keep moving towards Andalus!

One of the Iraqi soldiers told Salem and Yousef that he and seventeen of his friends wanted to desert the army but were afraid of what would happen to their families. He said they weren't the only ones who thought that the Kuwaitis didn't deserve what was happening to their country and that as soon as the first bullet was fired across the border a lot of Iraqis would immediately surrender!

There was a big explosion in Kheitan yesterday. Apparently the Iraqis had set up a market selling looted goods. The resistance blew it up.

Friday – Day 37

We're back home today. I was greeted like a long lost daughter by Salem's mother! Amazing what a war can do! It's nice to be back home though. Heather and Yousef are coming over for dinner tomorrow – I'm going to do steak and kidney pie! I wonder how long it will be before we eat that again! It won't be much longer before I'm eating rice everyday. The imported food supplies are running low. I'm looking forward to "Gulf

Link" on the World Service today and hope to hear about people we know. *Gulf Link is broadcast everyday by the World Service, airing messages from family and friends in England to those still in hiding in Kuwait.* We heard that the British convoy of people arrived back in London today. I hope Kathryn phones you soon.

Saturday – Day 38

A couple of nights ago a house on the road behind us which is brand new, and we thought uninhabited, was raided. Yesterday soldiers came to our house asking if we knew the people there and asking who lived in our house.

There seem to be more people staying in the house next door. It appears to be some sort of rest place for the officers. Every few days there is a change over.

We've got our answer phone rigged up now, but only one person so far has been brave enough to leave a message – Sami. He said he was thinking of driving to Baghdad to try and phone Emily. I expect Emily will have phoned you if he managed to speak to her.

Sunday – Day 39

The Bush/Gorbachov summit meeting is today.

I wonder if anything concrete will come out of it. Nothing very exciting happening so far today. I found an old book about palm reading. Heather and I had noticed that Saddam Hussein's two middle fingers are the same length. In the book it says that this indicates a gambler, someone who would gamble even with life itself! Interesting isn't it. All of us have a break in our life lines which indicates a major change or upheaval. They're right there!

Salem turned up with seven loaves of sliced bread yesterday, what a treat! That will keep me going for a while. Cigarettes are now only available on the black market at double the old price, which still isn't as much as they are in England!

Monday – Day 40

A boring day! I'm looking forward to my outing to Heather's this evening. Jamal went to collect Khawla and Naif from her mothers in Sabah Al Salem area but phoned to say they couldn't get back as they had sealed the whole area and were doing a house to house search.

Jassim came yesterday for one of his fleeting visits. He said that there is only one westerner left in Ahmadi, all the rest had been taken. I know some English girls married to Kuwaiti's living there – Jassim said that they took the women and the men were allowed to go with them if they chose.

Saddam Hussein is making a speech at six o'clock. Another rambling load of rubbish I expect!

Tuesday – Day 41

We've had confirmed reports that the Kuwait, Saudi and American troops that were in Wafra are now not far off Getty Beach area. The Iraqi's have been forced further back. Keep going! Keep going!

Jamal, Khawla and Naif managed to get here after all yesterday evening. Khawla's baby is due around the 18th and she is having a caesarean. There are about three hospitals that are still operating for the use of Kuwaiti's. Naif who is two years old, says the new baby is called Faisal Kuwaiti, NOT Faisal Iraqi! He also calls Saddam Hussein a donkey!

I wonder if Sally is getting married next week as expected.

I dreamt last night that both of you and Simon arrived on our doorstep with all your cases saying that you'd come to keep me company until the war was over. I was disappointed to wake up and find that you weren't there!

Wednesday – Day 42

Yesterday I heard a message on Gulf Link to Cathy and Alec, from Alec's Mum and Dad, so we presume that they are both still here. Salem has been trying to persuade me to leave with the next lot of women while I can. I don't want to go but I don't want to put Salem or his family in any danger by staying.

We've been having a bit of trouble with our daily visits to Heather and Yousef as they have been blocking the U turn at 9pm so that you have to go through the police check to get back. What a pain!

Bashar *(Salem's cousin)* has started a little video club with a collection of videos that are being lent out. I've got a nice horror film for Heather and I to watch today so I hope Heather can get out. Unfortunately there's only about fifteen English films in the collection, it won't take us long to get through those!

There is a new rule that all the Kuwaiti's must shave off their beards in the next two days or else have them shaved off forcibly. I've already given Salem his shaving orders! *It is common for*

Kuwaitis to grow their beards at times of sadness and with so many doing it, it had become an annoyance and symbol of passive resistance to the Iraqis. Also the pictures of the Emir and Crown Prince have to come down and Kuwaiti flags are banned. The penalty for failing to obey is execution. Charming!

Thursday – Day 43

Heather and I are reduced to writing letters to each other now. Heather, who knows how forgetful Salem is, even put a pin in her letter, hoping that Salem would put the letter in his pocket, sit on it and the pin would remind him to give it to me!

Salem went to the co-op today for me. I gave him a list but of course he couldn't get the imported stuff I wanted. In lieu of what he couldn't get I got four packets of spaghetti and three jars of jam! That should make an interesting meal!

Friday – Day 44

I'm getting increasingly concerned about Salem's mother's determination to leave Kuwait. She is now being supported by cousin Faisal and his wife Nawal, who heard yesterday that you could leave over the Saudi border again. Sometimes I feel I'm far more patriotic than they are. I'm very unhappy at the thought of getting up and leaving everything that I've put the last ten years of my life into. Apart from that, how am I going to get everything into one suitcase! Deciding what to leave and take would be heartbreaking. I just can't survive without my microwave and CD player for a start!

If only the rest of the world would start the attack then we'd have no choice. Contrary to what the World Service seems to think, most people here (apart from Salem's mother) want a war and want it NOW. As the days go by Iraq is getting more and more control over Kuwait, Saddam Hussein is slowly gaining more support with his propaganda and before long it will be too late.

Khawla has gone into hospital today and will be having a caesarean tomorrow. She had to go to a private hospital as the Iraqis have removed all the equipment from the government hospitals. Salem's Mum came up a little while ago and managed to thoroughly depress me. However much I tried to cheer her up she said that there was no chance for Kuwait and that we had to leave as soon as possible. In the end I told her that if she wanted to go she should, as it was no good being so depressed all the time and making everyone else depressed too! *This was the first time that I had spoken back to Salem's mother and it was actually a turning point in our relationship. When she discovered that I did not take the first opportunity to leave Kuwait, it finally dawned on her that I was in Kuwait because I loved her son. Now that I felt I had nothing left to lose I actually told her what I thought for a change and haven't looked back since.*

I've now settled down to knitting a little jumper for the new arrival – it might end up a bit multi-coloured if I don't have enough wool!

Saturday – Day 45

Khawla has had a boy; mother and baby are doing fine. They are going to call him Salem, isn't that nice! There were two British couples also at the hospital that had just produced girls. They were accompanied by their Iraqi guards.

We had a message from Sonia and Terry on Gulf Link yesterday....fantastic! I sit glued to it every night just in case, and when you actually hear your name you can't quite believe it!

Well it looks like I might be able to deliver this

letter personally soon. They've had confirmation that it's possible to get out through the Saudi border. It means I'll have to go on one of the flights out and as soon as Salem gets to Saudi he'll fly to London too. God knows what we'll do then, penniless, possessionless and jobless. We don't have much choice I suppose. Salem's gone to try and persuade Yousef and his Mum to join them, and Heather to join me. I don't know whether he'll have much success.

It's going to be very hard leaving all my treasures behind. I suppose I'll just bring winter clothes and that's it.

Sunday – Day 46

It looks as if we have to go now, whether we like it or not. Bloody Faisal (sorry Mum) and his wives have got us into all sorts of trouble. He is here with Nawal (the one you met) but is still married to Aisha (an Iraqi who is related to half the Iraqi army). Aisha was here a few days ago and then left. I don't know what happened between her and Faisal but she left their daughter behind, who I'm not very happy with as she got into our fridge and worked her way through most of the chocolate supplies! Last night around 12.20 Faisal had an anonymous phone call telling him to take care and get his family away safe as his wife is saying that everyone with Faisal is in the resistance. I don't have to tell you what the army does to resistance people. What with this and a mother-in-law who makes you whisper when you talk in case the soldiers hear you and has completely covered the windows in cellotape, in case of nerve gas, I'm pretty fed up!! You can imagine what sort of state poor Salem is in. They're all looking to him for a solution and nag him constantly. Mother-in-law wants to leave, granddad wants to stay. Whatever he says someone yells at him. As Jamal says the problem is that Salem's Mum has no courage, and fear is very infectious.

What a day! The decision was made, we were going. I'd packed all our worldly goods and taken all the food over to Heathers and was ready to say our goodbyes. Yousef and Salem popped over to the diwaniya and came back to say that all the plans were off! Because of, guess who....bloody Faisal (sorry again Mum!). Having stirred up the whole family all week into leaving, when we were ready to go he decides it's not a good idea after all! On leaving the country you have to hand over your passport, I.D., car registration, house deeds and sign a paper saying that you have no possessions in Kuwait. It is very final. I'm so relieved that we're not going, apart from leaving everything behind, I'd have to desert Heather. When we got back Aisha was there and apparently everything has been sorted out now, so we're OK on that score. Salem is relaxing for the first time this week.

Monday – Day 47

Well, thank goodness we didn't go this morning. They've announced on Voice of America that Westerners are not allowed out via Saudi Arabia. It would probably have meant that Salem and I would have had to have come back on our own. They did say that eight thousand Kuwaitis left yesterday and more are expected to go today which is a bit unnerving. I phoned the Embassy warden this morning to tell him that I wasn't going after all. He was very pleased to hear it but had to dash as his area was under threat of house to house search. I hope he's not found, he's been absolutely marvellous.

We were pleased to hear a message for Alex, from Pat on Gulf Link yesterday. I'm sure Pat will have phoned you and Heather's Mum when she got back. The message was to wish Alex a Happy

50th Birthday. They were planning on celebrating in Cyprus and I bet he didn't expect to have an alcohol free birthday!

They've just said on the news that people leaving for the Saudi border today had had the men taken by the Iraqis and the women sent on to Saudi. I'm SO glad we didn't go today!

Emily's friend Diana and her children are leaving on the next evacuation flight out, organized by the American Embassy, so I'll give this to her to send to you.

TO BE CONTINUED....

Tuesday 18th September – Day 48

I'm so pleased we managed to get our letters out. It should give you a few hours reading! Salem and Sami are pressuring me into leaving on the next flight out on Friday or Saturday. Salem still feels he should try to get his mother out before she cracks up completely! They have also heard of another route so maybe the women and men will travel separately. I don't really want to leave until they have some definite plans, on the other hand I don't want to be the one stopping them from going if they decide to leave at a later date.

Jamal received a letter, brought in by a friend,

from his mother, (who was in Jordan with his sister) saying that Salem's step-brother and sister and the rest of the family had arrived safely in Saudi Arabia and that they had joined them there.

I've just heard your message on Gulf Link and another one from Sonia and Terry and family! It's lovely to hear from you. I can't tell you what a difference it makes. Fortunately I recorded it so Salem can hear it too. He's popped down the road to his Uncles to see if there is any news and to get the gossip.

We've just heard that Diana is not going to leave after all. Apparently she didn't want to go anyway and having cried for two days she finally managed to persuade them to let her stay!

Wednesday – Day 49

A friend of Sami's who went up to the Saudi border and back again yesterday said that he saw with his own eyes Kuwaiti troops moving forward and Iraqis retreating! This is good! I wonder if they are acting on their own or if they have support from any other countries. In either case it might trigger something off to get things moving. Everyone feels that time is running out, especially now so many Kuwaitis are leaving.

Thursday – Day 50

Something very strange happened last night at 3.30am. Police cars were going up and down the road with their sirens blaring and loud speakers on telling all the lorries used for looting that were stopped overnight on the sides of the road to "Move out quickly. Get moving. As soon as possible leave". For about two hours we watched lorries moving out and hoped that this meant that finally something was going to happen. Unfortunately it seems to have been a false alarm as nothing has changed this morning.

Salem went shopping today and brought me a whole tray of eggs and fifty toilet rolls, what a luxury!

Friday – Day 51

We went over to Heather's yesterday evening and drove through the back way to avoid the road checks. We had to go where all the looting lorries were parked before they were moved on. They'd left hundreds of old flat tyres and the sand was scattered with the remains of water melons everywhere!

Salem's Mum, Sara and grandmother have spent the night over at Faisal's flat in Jabriya for the last couple of days, which was good for them as they are enclosed there and can't see what's going on. They can also get all the Gulf TV stations to watch instead of Iraqi propaganda. Unfortunately Faisal has again started stirring things up, after hearing the latest TV report from Iraq saying that they want a war, he's telling everyone that it is bound to happen in the next two days! This is not what Salem's Mum needs to hear!

Saturday – Day 52

Poor Salem had a terrible day yesterday. He had a row with Faisal for terrorizing his mother and told him to go and stay somewhere else, so he then had a row with his mother who didn't want Faisal to leave, as she feels safer with lots of men around. He went over to fetch Yousef to go shopping and Yousef's Mum turned on him for no apparent reason, and when he got home granddad had a go at him for coming home late! This waiting is driving everyone crazy!

As I write there has been another explosion down by the roundabout where all the soldiers on leave hang around waiting to hitch a lift. Lots of black smoke.

Sunday – Day 53

The other day Sami told me a funny story about a friend of his, which just goes to show how much law and order is breaking down. Hawalli is the area where all the Palestinians and Lebanese live. This man was in Hawalli when he had a flat tyre. While he was changing the wheel he felt the car rocking so went to have a look to see what was wrong, only to discover that another man was taking one of the other wheels off! When he told the man that it was his car and what did he think he was doing, he replied "OK, so you found it first, I'll take one wheel; you can take the other three"!

Tuesday – Day 55

Nothing very exciting happened yesterday, except Salem managed to find me three big jars of coffee and some salty butter! This morning they are moving all the lorries on again, but this time they have also stopped all the private cars from driving down to the roundabout, they are directing them all into Andalus. Only lorries (and there are hundreds of them) and military are allowed to go on the 4th ring road it seems. We think there might possibly be one of the organised demonstrations at the roundabout as there is a huge picture of Saddam Hussein there which is soon to be unveiled. Aren't we lucky!

We heard a message from Cathy's Mum and Dad on Gulf Link last night. I hope they are being kept in one of the Hotels in Baghdad and not at a military installation somewhere as Saddam's guests.

The Kuwaiti Dinar is no longer acceptable currency here, which doesn't really matter as I only have one and a quarter Dinars in my purse! Yousef's Mum went to the co-op and bought around KD. 5 worth of food and it only cost one Iraqi Dinar. The co-op by the way has been taken over by the Iraqis.

Wednesday – Day 56

Last night, around 10pm, police cars started moving all the trucks out again and at around midnight they moved them all back! It's driving Salem absolutely crazy, he's dying to know what they're up to! This morning, the house behind, which is occupied by Iraqi soldiers and Palestinians are moving all the furniture out of the house into the courtyard! I'd love to know what they're up to as well! Last night we had a really thick fog, something which I've only ever seen in Kuwait once before, we were hoping that the fog would disappear and take with it all the Iraqis.

LATER – a load of soldiers have just arrived next door with a big truck and taken all the furniture away, right down to the chandeliers and curtain rails.

Thursday – Day 57

They've cleared out the remaining furniture in next doors house although there still appear to be four people staying there. They found a can of green spray paint and have sprayed "Welcome" in Arabic on the wall next to the front door and something else all over the back of the gate. Charming isn't it. Thank goodness we didn't leave or all our furniture would be going out as well.

Friday – Day 58

Heather and Yousef are able to get some of the other Gulf stations on TV and recorded the Emirs speech at the United Nations for us. It had the whole family in tears. What a fantastic reception he had. This was something that they DIDN'T show on Iraqi TV – more's the pity!

We have been given one month to change our Identity Cards to Iraqi ones. Huh!!!

Saturday – Day 59

The soldiers occupying the house next door have finally gone, but not without setting fire to the house first. They broke all the windows and shot at the house until the fire really got underway. The fire brigade arrived but they sent them packing. They stopped the traffic coming anywhere near the house and told everyone that it was a resistance house. Amazing as there have been no Kuwaiti occupants since 3rd August! When they finally left the fire brigade came back to put out the fire. The last time I saw the fire brigade in action was when we lived in Nailsworth and those trees at the top of the garden caught fire! Exciting stuff eh!

Sunday – Day 60

A very boring day! Sod'ems speech was especially boring. Nothing new as usual.

Some quite bizarre things happen as a result of the invasion. We heard of a friend whose car had broken down on one of the motorways and as he tried to repair it a zebra walked by! As the zookeepers were forced to depart, rather than leave the animals to die in cages they released most of them hoping that they could fend for themselves. *The zookeepers weren't the only ones to release their captives as they abandoned their posts; prisoners were also released from their jail cells.*

Monday October 1st – Day 61

Sami came today with a cooler full of goodies for us, including a jar of salad cream. Oh for a lettuce! We are still able to get tomatoes so we're not completely saladless! But guess what else he brought....half a bottle of gin! Fantastic! *Being a Mulsim country, the sale of alcohol is forbidden in Kuwait. Now it's available everywhere and some enterprising Iraqis have set up their own stand selling alcohol on the roundabout down the road!*

Tuesday – Day 62

Well I was very restrained with the gin yesterday. I have a fear that the war will start and I'll have a dreadful hangover! It gave me strange dreams though. I was woken up by someone shouting my name!

There was another big explosion today down by the roundabout and they're moving all the trucks out again this evening.

There is an astrologer in Kuwait who predicted that 2nd August would begin a very bad time for

Kuwait. However, he did say that from 4th to 15th October would be a very happy time. Here's hoping!

Wednesday – Day 63

Heather and Yousef had a message on Gulf Link from her Mum and Dad yesterday. I got up early this morning to try and record the repeat of it for her but unfortunately the reception was so bad I couldn't get any of it. I'm so glad she heard from them, I think she was beginning to despair that they had completely disowned her.

Thursday – Day 64

Yesterday they showed on TV a video of Kuwait through someone's car window, all along the seafront and right down as far as Sulaibikhat. There was a big picture of Saddam Hussein in front of the towers and an amazing lack of traffic, and there were jumps in the film when they passed the British and American Embassies! Of course the towers weren't shown close enough for the blown out windows to show. They also interviewed a Yemeni man who said he had been tortured by the Saudis. They kept handing him a gottra* and every time they did so he kept crying

*The head covering worn by men

and used it to wipe away invisible tears!

The playing cards that you bought Salem for Christmas are practically worn out; everyone is playing endless games of patience with them!

We hear lots of horror stories but, touch wood, we don't seem to be getting much hassle from the troops in Andalus and the shooting that we used to hear most nights is now only about once a week or so. *Apart from the reports of terrible torture inflicted on the Kuwaiti's who are unlucky enough to be captured and interrogated, the story that sticks in my mind the most is this one. We heard of a Kuwaiti army officer who was found in his home with his wife and three daughters. The Iraqi's told him that if he didn't give them a certain amount of money for each of the women in his family then they would rape them. Everyone tried to get together as much money as they could in the short time they had been allowed and handed it over to the Iraqi officer. He said "You have saved your wife and two of your daughters". The soldiers raped his third daughter, while her father was forced to watch.*

Friday – Day 65

Well it looks like we might be leaving again. The news that there will be another flight out next week has just increased the odds. Faisal has one plan, Salem has another. On past experience Salem is concentrating on his plan! Salem and Sami have gone to see a man this afternoon. *This man lives next to the Iranian Embassy and is providing fake Iranian I.D.'s. They then drive everyone in a bus through Iraq and out over the Iranian border. I've been searching through the photos for a picture of Salem in a shirt without a tie (as the Iranian's do not wear ties) and managed to find one that will do. He should come back with an I.D., with a new Iranian name and the occupation of a carpenter!* We'll see what happens next. I've got that sinking feeling in my stomach again when I think of leaving this place.

Saturday – Day 66

Well the events of last night have made the decision to leave a bit easier. At 12.30am there were suddenly around twenty soldiers outside. They had the house surrounded. They came in one car and two trucks. They were ready to come in but Faisal and another man (an old friend of the family) dashed outside. I hurriedly got dressed and was about to don my abaya and go and try and be inconspicuous amongst the rest of the women downstairs, but by this time they had started to leave. They wanted to know why there were so many cars coming and going to our house. The main reason, of course, is that Faisal invites all his friends over, and yesterday, what with all the plans for leaving going on, various different people were visiting who wanted to join them. After last night it's fairly certain that the Iraqis will be keeping an eye on this house, so we may even move out sooner than Wednesday.

LATER. Well I'm booked on Wednesday's flight and all the plans are going ahead. This evacuation, unlike the previous ones, will not fly out of Kuwait airport as the resistance recently shot down an Iraqi aircraft nearby. We will go by coach to Basra and fly back to England from there. Most of the family will be going the day after tomorrow and the rest, Salem and Sami will follow as soon as I'm on the plane. I wish Heather was coming with me, I don't relish telling Heather's Mum that I'm home and Heather's not. I think Yousef would like her to go, maybe there's still time to persuade her.

Salem got told off at the police check today for sitting with his legs crossed! That's a new rule!

Sunday – Day 67

There's a police check at the end of the road

today, right outside Uncles house, so it doesn't look like I'm going to get to see Heather before I leave at this rate. She's very kindly offered to look after all my treasures for me. We'll just have to take our chances with the rest of the stuff in the house. One thing's for sure, they'll never get the pool table out! The British Embassy is going to get a message out to you to let you know I'm coming on the Wednesday flight.

Apparently the Hilton was blown up last night by the resistance. They still seem to be active. There was shooting going on up the road last night as well. I don't know what all that was about.

Diana and her five children will be on the same flight as me. She's now leaving after all.

Yousef's Mum has decided that if there's a war then they all have to sit under the stairs with saucepans on their heads for protection! I can just picture it! We have heard that this morning a man was shot right outside their house. Maybe that will persuade them to leave. Salem will no doubt hear about it when he goes there later.

Monday – Day 68

Apparently the son of the people who live in the house opposite Heather's had been picked up for questioning weeks ago. Yesterday morning they brought him back, called his family to the door then shot him dead in front of them. They were told not to touch his body for twenty four hours so that everyone could see what happened to those in the resistance. *His body was covered in scars from torture; he had no fingernails and was covered in burn marks.* This sort of event is getting more and more frequent. Unfortunately it still hasn't changed Heather and Yousef's minds.

The family's plans seem to change by the hour. There's a family meeting later today to come to a final decision. I hate the waiting now. I've been wondering whether I should take things, hide them or send them over to Heather's.

Nawal's mother and the women of her family left today for Saudi.

Well almost 50 pages…not quite a book, but it might make interesting reading. I'm glad I did write this letter as I'm sure I'd never have remembered everything that happened. I'm pleased to be able to deliver this to you personally and put your minds at rest but I'm heartbroken to be leaving Kuwait not knowing when and in what circumstances I'll return. I shall be desperately worried until I know that everyone is safe and I hate leaving friends behind.

Love Karen

Karen Alanizi

THE JOURNEY HOME

Well this is it. The decision has finally been made. I'm going home. I'm allowed one suitcase and I spend hours wandering around the house trying to decide what to take with me. All the time thinking that this will probably be the last time I will ever see my home of the last three years and my adopted country for the last ten. When it comes down to it, all the things of sentimental value that I have become so attached to are left behind. I pack warm clothes for the coming winter in England and things of value that I can sell if I need to. The American Embassy informed us that it is safe to take jewellery, but not to take cameras or film as the Iraqi's see these as a threat to their security. I retrieve the jewellery that was hidden buried in the plant pot and pack it into my vanity case along with Salem's prized diamond Cartier watch, which he insists I take. I also secrete a roll of film, wrapped in socks and stuffed well into the bottom of a pair of boots at the bottom of my suitcase. They contain pictures taken from the windows .... as the tanks arrived, as they set up camp on the land next to us and as they took up residence in the neighbours house, before finally looting and burning it.

This is the hardest day of my life and as it gets late we go to bed to try and get some sleep. We cling to each other not knowing how long it will be before we see each other again and I feel Salem's body shudder as he sobs that he is losing everything......his country, his freedom and now me. It's the first time I've ever seen him cry and I can't keep it in any longer. The tears flow and we cry together in each others arms, not knowing what the future holds for us, and praying that we will be together again soon. Eventually we drift into a restless sleep and all too soon it is morning and time to leave. I'm so grateful to Sami who has very kindly offered to take me to the collection point at Safeway supermarket car park in Farwaniya. If the Iraqi's are watching the house and searching for Marwan it will be safer for Salem to stay out of sight for the time being. I put on my borrowed abaya and start my goodbyes. As

Sara hugs me close and wishes me a safe journey she tells me to send a radio message to let them know that I've arrived safely. It doesn't dawn on me until later that if they are leaving tomorrow, as planned, then there would be no point as they won't be here to hear it.

We set off on the fifteen minute journey to Safeway and for the first time in two and a half months I get to venture further than Andalus and see how dense the occupation has become. There are Iraqi check points everywhere, every school, every government building and every abandoned house has been taken over and occupied. Sami reminds me to leave my Civil I.D. card behind, which has my address on it, and we secrete it in his father's car, where forgotten, it remains until after the liberation. We arrive without incident and I shed the abaya and join the crowds of people waiting by the coaches.

Most western women have already left Kuwait and the coaches are full of Arabs of dual nationality, mostly men and a few women, who have American passports. Most of them did not follow the one suitcase rule and it's chaos as people jostle to get their luggage on board. I spot Diana and her children in the crowds but we get separated as we are sorted on to the buses. I end up sitting near two British ladies, wives of military men, who have new born babies and a small child with them. They are the same ladies that Salem met in the hospital when Khawla had her baby. Next to me sits Carol. She's an American, about eight months pregnant, married to a Palestinian. She has a bruised face where her husband has beaten her and then kicked her out of the house, presumably afraid that he would be accused of harbouring a westerner if caught by the Iraqis. She had taken refuge at the American Embassy who had arranged for her to leave. Her perspective on the situation is completely different to ours. Having lived with a Palestinian family she sees the Iraqis as friends and liberators.

We eventually set off in convoy and instead of heading for the Iraqi border go in the opposite direction, which causes some concern. We come to a halt in the car park of the Hyatt Regency Hotel, where all the captured westerners were being held. Iraqi soldiers board the bus and question us individually. What's my name? Who's my husband? Where is he now? I tell them that I have no idea where my husband is and that I haven't seen him for months. Carol can't understand why I'm lying to them; she has no idea of the threats against the Kuwaitis. Though some remained loyal to Kuwait the majority of Palestinians worked with the Iraqis and also shared in their spoils. I try to enlighten her as to some of the horrific events that the Iraqis and Palestinians are responsible for.

Two men are taken off the bus but later return and then we are on our way, this time in the right direction. I am hoping to take the road that leads past our house, but we take the 6th Ring road that runs parallel to it, and I don't get to see my home one last time. I suddenly have a thought. Today is the 10th October, ten years exactly to the day that I met Salem. I think back to when we met. I was the catering manager of a private boy's boarding school in the countryside of Surrey. We got up very early in the mornings and our evening entertainment rarely meant venturing much further than the local pub. It was Jenny's birthday and we asked her what she would like to do to celebrate. "Go dancing!" was the reply. So a grand night out in Guildford was planned and with Jenny wearing her "Its My Birthday Be Nice To Me" badge, a group of us set off for Cinderella Rockerfellas. Salem was a student at Wimbledon

College at the time and had gone to visit a friend at his home in Wokingham. His home, I later found out, used to belong to Tom Jones and was a huge mansion! The friend was a member of the exiled ruling family of Libya! They also decided to go somewhere new and ended up in Guildford. As we bought our drinks and went to sit down we were told by Salem that we were sitting in their place! We were about to move when Salem noticed Jenny's birthday badge and insisted on buying her a drink and letting us share their seats. The rest is history. We became engaged on Valentines day, or more appropriately "Volunteers Day" as Salem once mispronounced it! By April we were married and living in Kuwait. And here I am ten years later, reluctantly sitting on a coach that is taking me away from him.

As we pass the Mutla Ridge I notice the bomb damaged communications dishes and it is around lunchtime by the time we reach the Safwan border post. Most of us have brought something to eat and drink and we share it amongst us. The bus driver even passes around some sweets! We stay at the border for hours and are not allowed to get off the bus. Poor Carol is desperate to use the bathroom and in the end has to make use of the back seat which is fortunately unoccupied. We don't make a move until it gets dark and as we travel I notice that the street lamps are not lit. There must be something here that we are not meant to see. Finally we arrive at Basra Airport where our cases are searched. While my case is opened at one desk I am called to another to have my vanity bag searched. They take everything out and talk to me from both desks distracting my attention. Although I don't notice then, it must have been at this time that Salem's beloved watch disappeared. One of the girls with the new baby has a video camera secreted in her suitcase. Having never seen one before they ask her what it is and when she tells them it is something for the baby, they happily accept her story and let her keep it!

The next stage is to "check in". We have to show our passports at a desk where an overly friendly soldier with excellent English claims that he knew my husband when he was in Kuwait and then tries to pry information about him out of me. Again I use the "I know nothing" approach. In order to get through passport control we have to have a red triangular exit stamp imprinted on our passport. The man wielding the stamp, finding himself with this sudden unexpected power, starts shouting orders at us. "Sit on the Floor!", "Do not Speak!" But as more and more people begin to filter through from the first passport check the area gets fuller and fuller and he has to start using his stamp and letting people through. I manage to find the two English girls and their children and we finally find bathrooms and there is even a cafeteria open. Salem has given me some Iraqi Dinars so we buy a welcome beer and sandwich to keep us going.

When we board the plane we assume that we are heading for London but a short time later we are descending into Baghdad Airport, where we are ordered to leave everything on the plane and disembark for a photo opportunity! Saddam Hussein wants us shown on TV, as proof of his generosity at letting us leave! I help the girl who has the small child by carrying the new born baby in my arms and when arriving in a cordoned off area flooded with lights and cameras, am greeted by the British Ambassador to Iraq who asks me if I have enough nappies! I have to tell him that this isn't even my baby and wonder what my friends and family in England are thinking if this is being aired on TV there! Half an hour later and we are back on board, the infant sound asleep as I hand him back to his mother. Finally we are on our way. They serve us some hummus with frankfurters in it, not very appetizing! Seven hours later we touch down at Gatwick and the steward announces "Welcome to Gatwick Airport, we hope you enjoyed your flight and look forward to seeing you on Iraqi Airlines again"! This is acknowledged by some very tired sounding jeers!

As we walk down the steps of the plane and the cold autumn air hits our faces the Red Cross are there with blankets and we are guided into a private reception area where we collect our cases and are greeted by a wonderful lady with a cockney accent, offering us hot tea and sandwiches. The relief is palpable but I feel strangely numb and quite stunned by the fact that everything is so normal here while there is so much suffering going on in Kuwait......and I feel guilty that I have left it all behind, along with my husband and friends. While I am now secure in my homeland and soon to be in the loving arms of my family, their futures are uncertain.

We are invited to have a brief word with the Ministry of Defence, who take contact details so that they can interview us at a later date, in case we have any information that may be of value. We are offered the help of the social services and as I am fortunate enough to be married to a Kuwaiti I'm told to go and register at Kuwait Airways in London and they will give me some financial aid. I later discover that whereas other nationalities were presented with a bill for their return flight home, the Kuwaiti government covered all my expenses, for which I am truly grateful.

We are told that a private room is ready for us to meet our loved ones, and as we exit the building an interview area has been set up by the press, if we wish to speak to them. A member of the airport staff has already made an emotional announcement to our families that we have touched down safely and that they will be seeing us soon. I'm exhausted now, I've been awake for over 24 hours but all tiredness leaves me as I walk into the room and see the faces of my Mum and Dad. Before I can reach them I'm engulfed in my brother's red and white anorak as he comes from nowhere to give me a hug. It's so good to see them. We walk past the cameras and get on a coach to take us to the car park. I start to tell them some of the things that are happening in Kuwait, though I don't really know where to start, and a TV crew hold up a microphone to the window to try and catch some of our conversation. I keep telling them that Salem is coming soon, that he should be on his way right now. I don't know how wrong I am.

WAITING

I spend the next few days staying at Simon and Jane's house in Stevenage. Mum and Dad have already put five hundred pounds in my account so that I don't have to worry about money, bless them. I go into London and find my way to Kuwait Airways. It's the strangest feeling seeing all these Kuwaiti's seemingly without a care in the world. A Ferrari pulls up on the double yellow lines outside and the occupant comes in to collect his monthly cheque and presumably is off to spend it immediately on having a good time. I want to scream at them.....don't you know what's happening to your fellow countrymen.....how dare you enjoy yourself while they're suffering! I feel close to tears as I give my details to the receptionist who shortly after hands me a cheque. They arrange to transfer five hundred pounds every month into my account. Those Kuwaitis who have to find somewhere to live are also paid an accommodation allowance on top of this. I silently thank the government of Kuwait, now exiled in Taif in Saudi Arabia, for looking after me so well. At least that's one less thing to worry about.

The Kuwaitis are extremely fortunate in that the oil wealth has made life very easy for them. The late Emir, Sheikh Jaber Al Sabah certainly looked after his subjects and I'm sure that his successor will continue to do so. There is no income tax. Education is free up to University level including an allowance for students at higher levels. Medical and dental services are free and if they are unable to treat you in Kuwait, you and a member of your family will be sent abroad with all expenses paid. Newly weds receive an eight thousand pound gift to help them get started (unfortunately Salem and I did not qualify for this as I was a foreigner!). Every married couple is entitled to choose between a ready built government house or a plot of land and a grant with which to build their own property. The money for this is paid back over several years by extremely low monthly payments.

The Emir often makes a financial gift,

Letter Home

sometimes up to four hundred pounds to every Kuwaiti on the occasion of Eid* and after the liberation all loans taken by nationals were cancelled. When I tell a Kuwaiti that in England you have to buy a licence if you want to own a television, and pay road tax if you own a car, I'm looked at in utter disbelief!

We get back home to Saltford where my Dad has raised the Kuwaiti flag from the flag pole in the garden. It stays there until liberation. Mum has kept all the letters from well wishers for me to read. They are from relatives, their friends and mine. I start to read them and am overcome with emotion to find that so many people have been thinking of us and care enough to write. I have to stop or I will breakdown completely. I don't get around to reading them until well after liberation and years later still find them very emotional. There are also newspaper cuttings. My Dad had a letter printed in the Daily Express which he had written after they had published headlines saying that Saddam will turn Kuwait into a graveyard. He thought that this kind of reporting showed a lack of sensitivity to the families and friends of those

---

*A Muslim holiday celebrated at the end of Ramadan and at the end of the annual pilgrimage to Mecca.

trapped in Kuwait. This letter sparked a flurry of phone calls from television news channels, national and local newspapers and local radio stations. It became so frequent that they kept handy a prepared standard reply to read out to all the enquiries, stating that they had no comment to make.

I discovered that all those friends that had left Kuwait saying that they would contact my parents had kept their promises and passed on our messages as soon as they had arrived. I too had called our wardens family to pass on their message and had spoken to Heather's parents too. Emily had also been calling Mum and Dad on a regular basis. I let her know that Sami was safe and sound and that he was planning to leave with Salem and his family.

I'm so proud of my parents. I discover that they volunteered to man the phones at the Gulf Support Group Help Line, which was set up in Bristol by a local MP. Having been to Kuwait several times they were able to help many people who were concerned about their loved ones trapped there and had no idea what the country was actually like. Dad had a map of Kuwait which he lent to them and it was pinned up on the wall and often appeared on the local TV news reports. In the first few days of it being set up they manned the phones on several occasions. They remembered one girl who was very concerned about the safety of her boyfriend. When my Dad asked her where he was she replied that he was on the USS Enterprise in the Suez Canal. Dad told her that if he wasn't safe there he wouldn't be safe anywhere! There were other calls from people who had no idea of the location of their loved ones other than a Post Office Box address. My parents did a great job offering words of comfort until the whole operation was moved up to London.

Dad comes back from the Post Office up the road to say that a friend he bumped into, enquired about us and was almost brought to tears with the news that I was back safe and sound. Complete strangers come up to me in the street and grab hold of me saying how happy they are that I'm back. I'm happy too but I'm aching inside....still no word from Salem. I now really appreciate what I put my family through by not leaving Kuwait earlier. I knew I was OK in Kuwait but they had no idea what was happening and the not knowing is the hardest thing of all. Every time the phone rings my stomach leaps. This must be Salem, he should be out by now. What could have happened? My mind runs riot, hoping for the best and imagining the worst. I don't realize now that the sound of that particular ring, years later, will take me instantly back to this time and this awful feeling.

I call Gulf Link and send my message through to Salem and to Heather and Yousef to let them know that I have got back safely. I manage to express my profound thanks to the organisers of Gulf Link and let them know how much it means to the British people in Kuwait receiving the messages. A few days letter I become brave enough to do a recorded message to everyone and start off with "Get those saucepans off your heads there's a message coming through!", hopefully sounding a lot cheerier than I actually feel.

I have become addicted to the news and when not reading the papers sit glued to the television. One evening the local news channel interviews a teenager who tells the story of how he escaped by getting a fake Iranian ID and getting out through Iran. I scream at the television in despair as he tells the world, and the Iraqis, how my husband is planning to get back to me. I'm convinced that this will now put a stop to this route and I will never see Salem again.

The roll of film has been developed and the situation becomes more real to my family as they see everything in relation to our house and the places that they recognize. The Ministry of Defence send a man round to talk to me. He's delighted with the photos and although some of them show pictures of tanks in the far distance he assures me that they can easily magnify them to see what they are. He asks me a lot of questions, shows me pictures of different kinds of helicopters, tanks and missile launchers for me to try and recognise. I do my best but it's difficult and I wish that I'd taken more notice of everything that I'd seen. As I speak I feel myself shaking inside and wonder if it notices in my voice. He's very interested in the destroyed communication dishes that I saw at Mutla ridge and I realize how difficult it is to judge size and distance. He takes the negatives and promises that he will return them after they have been analyzed.

The Free Kuwait Campaign is already well underway and I discover that the Bath area branch is being run by an Al-Anizi family who were living in the area at the time the invasion happened. I call them to see if there is anything that I can do to show my support and they invite me to their home to discuss their plans for the next day of action. Every second of the month, in recognition of the date of the invasion they take to the streets to remind people what is happening thousands of miles away. Dad drives me over in the evening and in typical Kuwaiti style he is whisked upstairs to the makeshift diwaniya with all the men and I am taken to sit with the ladies. They come from Sulaibikhat, not far from Andalus and are desperate for any news that I can give them. I do the best that I can, although not having been out very much there's not a lot I can tell them about their area. At the end of the evening I manage to talk briefly with the men and I'm given the area around the Bath bus station to go and distribute "Free Kuwait" badges and flyers.

It feels good to be doing something positive. I want to tell everyone what's going on in Kuwait but most people just take the badges and hurry on their way. Some take the time to listen to you and most are supportive and horrified at the stories that we have to tell. On the way home a gypsy woman stops me and asks me to buy a bunch of lavender. Normally I would say no, but I'm not taking any chances, I'll accept all the luck I can get and I certainly don't need any curses put on me!

I never understood how people could become so depressed that they don't want to do anything but feel sorry for themselves. Now I understand. I cry myself to sleep every night and start all over again in the morning when I awake to the realization that I still have no news of Salem. Out of the blue I suddenly burst into tears and although I can cope very well with discussing the facts of the invasion with all those kind enquiring friends, I can't cope at all when people are nice to me.

I want to go back to Kuwait. I picture myself on the M4 motorway with a hitchhikers sign saying "Kuwait City". I just want to find out what has happened and why Salem hasn't contacted me.

It is simply the presence of my parents that prevents me from staying in bed all day and drinking myself into oblivion. Something has to be done. I decide to try and find work. Not only will it help with the finances but it will give me something else to think about. I go into the Job Centre in Bath and find temporary part time employment in a card and gift shop. It's great. Lovely people to work with and so hectic that we don't stop all day. It's just what I need. I'm too busy to think.

Christmas is getting closer and everywhere is looking very festive. Mum and Dad go out one Friday evening to help prepare the local hall for the annual Christmas event and I'm on my own for the first time since I returned. The phone rings. That familiar feeling fills my guts and I pick it up readying myself for the usual disappointment and over a crackly line....... I hear Salem's voice. He's in Saudi Arabia at the border! I can't stop crying with relief and he begs me to stop as he's struggling to hold back his own tears. It's only because he happens to know the man at the Saudi holding post that he manages to get him to allow him to make a call. Thank you! Thank you! Thank you! Our conversation is brief, everyone is OK but Grandad is not with them, he wouldn't leave, and neither is Sami. He promises to call me again as soon as he can.

I'm so relieved, the longest six weeks of my life is finally over. I cry some more and when my parents return they're overjoyed to hear the news. He's safe and he's out of Kuwait. Now I just want him back here with me and I wait excitedly for the next phone call.

I call Emily with the news that Salem is back and hold back my euphoria as I have to break the news to her that Sami is not with him.

The second of December arrives and I decide to join an organised march through the streets of London ending in Trafalgar Square. I meet up with Emily and we collect our Free Kuwait placards and join the thousands of people marching. It's good to see some familiar faces and wonderful to discover so many British people marching alongside the Kuwaiti's, supporting the cause.

It's not long before I hear from Salem again. Having gone through all the formalities of getting through the border procedures they are now heading for Jeddah where they have relations. It seems to take forever for Salem to get his family settled and then he has to persuade the Kuwaiti authorities in Saudi Arabia to send him to England. This involves several frantic phone calls to various officials trying to prove that he is my husband and that I desperately need him to come to England to look after me! Finally they agree and having spent Christmas at Jane's parents in

Derby we go back to my brother's place in Stevenage to await Salem's arrival. He arrives, via Rome at Heathrow at 5.30 on the morning of 28th December. I'm so nervous as the arrivals board show that the plane has landed, the waiting seems to go on forever. Suddenly he's there, walking down the centre of the arrivals hall and I'm in his arms, holding on to him for dear life. Thank you God!

Of course my first question is why didn't you leave the day after me, as planned? Over the next few days I get to hear the whole story. Some of which chills me to the bone.

SALEMS STORY

The day after I left, the family decided to wait until they got a message from me through Gulf Link to ensure that I had got home safely. Salem felt a lot freer and able to move around, without having to worry about getting back to check that I was OK all the time. He spent time at his Uncles house, at the diwaniya (which I now discover was the local resistance headquarters), at Sami's and visiting Heather and Yousef to check up on the Gulf Link messages. He felt that each day might be the day that the Liberation of Kuwait would begin and he wanted to be there for it.

One evening in late November the door bell rang. Salem went to answer it and saw a man, Ali that used to work for Marwan, with two other men who were wearing dishdashas and gottras, but without egals*. They had come in a car with a

*The black rope circle worn on the head on top of the gottra.

broken side window and Ali was looking extremely uneasy. Salem suspected that the car was stolen and that the two strangers were Iraqis but nonetheless invited them in. The two men declined but Ali followed Salem into the big reception hall downstairs. He sat very close to Salem and whispered to him that he and his brother had been taken by the Iraqis but that he had been released. While he was in custody he had seen a file with a list of names. Salem's name was on it. He told Salem that he should leave as soon as possible before they came to take him.

Salem called Jamal and they discussed it with another friend Mahmoud whose wife, Sausan was Sara's friend. They had already decided that if the time came they would all leave together. They didn't want to give up and go but decided that they would think about it and make a decision later. They buried all the weapons in the garden just in case the house was searched. Salem and Jamal thought it would be wise to keep away from the house and moved in with Sami and his family for a few days to see what happened. In case their names were already on an arrest list they travelled to Sami's house trying to avoid check points and were armed with packets of cigarettes to use as bribes if necessary.

A few days passed and they decided to go back home. No-one had been to the house looking for them so they relaxed a bit. Salem went to see Heather and Yousef and they gave him a cassette that they had recorded with the Gulf Link messages on it.

He got home just as it was getting dark, around 7pm, and joined his family who were watching the news in the small sitting room at the front of the house. Suddenly they heard shouting outside. Sara looked out of the window and simply said "They came".

Soldiers were on top of the mulhaq, a building which ran along the side of the house which had a diwaniya at the front and a kitchen and living quarters for the housemaids and driver. There were more soldiers in trucks outside who started to get out and surround the house. They rang the door bell and before Salem answered it he threw his notebook, holding all his important contact phone numbers into the bushes in the garden. They wanted to know if he was Marwan and then forced themselves inside the house. Three men in civilian clothes demanded to know where Marwan was and to know who else was in the house. Sara started to yell insults at them and insulted Saddam Hussein at which point they grabbed hold of Salem, held a gun to his head and released the safety catch, telling her to keep quiet. Salem's mother started begging them not to shoot him and went to kiss the soldiers hand, pleading for her son's life. Salem couldn't bear the shame of seeing his mother behaving this way towards a man that was their enemy and pushed her away. Things began to calm down as the women became silent and the men were moved into the big reception room. Salem, Granddad, Uncle, Faisal, Jamal and a friend of granddads who was visiting, all waited nervously to see what would happen next.

The soldiers asked who everyone was. They said that they knew that Marwan was still in Kuwait and that they took him food everyday! The three Iraqi's and some soldiers began to search the house with Uncle and the rest of the men were sent to wait in the back of one of the trucks. The truck had gravel on the bottom of it and they were forced to crouch in the cold for two and a half hours while they searched every room in the house. Granddad shook with the cold. Sara's friend Sausan phoned her to say that she was coming over to visit and, as she was being closely observed, Sara told her not to come as Grandmother was ill and all the men were taking her to the hospital. Sausan understood immediately what had happened and warned her husband. They allowed the women to come out and talk to the men in the truck and eventually the search was finished and uncle came back. They took Salem back into the house and began to question him. Why were there so many cars at the house? Salem's Porsche had been hidden in the garage at the back of the house as most up-market cars were confiscated at the Iraqi check points. My car was in the front of the house, along with cars belonging to each of the men and Sara. He wanted to know if any of them were government cars and then asked where the guns were hidden. Thank goodness they had buried them in the garden, days before. He insisted that they must be resistance as they had a typewriter in the house that must be used for typing messages to other resistance members! Salem told them that they had brought it from the office and that they were no threat to them.

Half an hour later they returned Salem to the truck and Mahmoud, Sara's son aged seven who was going through a superman phase and was afraid of nothing, came running out towards them. The soldiers pushed him away and Mahmoud hit at the handcuffs on the soldiers belt shouting that he was not the only one with handcuffs, his uncle had some too!! Mahmoud meant his Uncle Marwan in the police force but the Iraqis assumed he meant Salem. So Salem was taken back inside once again and was pushed and shoved around while they demanded to know where the handcuffs were. Salem said that Mahmoud was just a boy and he was probably just talking about toys, so they went to Mahmoud's room, which was piled high with games and toys of every kind and fortunately found a box with two pairs of plastic handcuffs in it. What a relief.

They put Salem back in the truck and as they drove away Salem looked into his mother's eyes and knew that he would see her again.

They were taken to the police station in Ardiya, the area next to Andalus and put into a room where they were left alone for a while. Salem remembered that he still had the cassette in his pocket and also some Kuwaiti money, which was now illegal and an offence to carry. He quickly slid them under the cushion of the bench they were sitting on.

Uncle was the first to be called into the interrogation room. They could hear the discussion through the door and they just kept asking the same questions, wanting to know where Marwan was and why Uncle was in our house. Meanwhile a man dressed in jeans and carrying a machine gun came and sat directly opposite Salem and with knees almost touching stared directly at him, saying nothing.

They asked if they could use the bathroom and were told to all go together!

Faisal was questioned next and granddad recognized the man doing the questioning as a man that had come to the house before saying that he was doing a survey and wanting to know who was in the house. One by one they were taken in and asked the same questions. Thankfully they were not tortured. Some pushing, shoving and slapping, but no damage really done. Eventually the men were released......except Salem and Jamal, who were put into jail. They were told that in exchange for a TV or VCR they could be released! We had two VCR's at home ready for this kind of occasion, but as events unfolded they weren't needed at this time. They were however used at a later date to release someone else! A neighbour came to the police station to ask about them but was told that they had been moved to a different place.

Suddenly in the early hours of the morning they grabbed hold of Salem and Jamal and put them back in the truck. They told them they were going to be released. They felt very uneasy, things didn't seem right, and as they took them back to the house and stopped the truck on the empty land about seventy metres from the house they became more and more fearful that, as had happened to so many others before them, they would be shot in the back before they reached home. Instinctively they grabbed hold of each other's arms as they walked slowly away, so that they would feel who would be first to fall. Those seventy metres felt like miles. The truck drove away and with a sigh of relief they made it back inside the house and shut the door.

Marwan had warned Salem, before he left, of the way the Iraqi's operated. Once you had been arrested your file would then be handed on to the Mukhabarat, Saddams Secret Service Officers, who were well known for their torture tactics and from whom few people ever returned alive. They must leave....and as soon as possible.

They quickly packed a few belongings into the cars. Sara, who was expecting a baby made the difficult decision of leaving her husband behind who had decided to stay with his family in Ahmadi. Granddad refused to leave along with the two housemaids, who since the beginning of the invasion had insisted on staying with the family rather than go to their embassy to be evacuated.

Salem was proud of his grandfather's courage in staying but also envied him. He didn't want to leave but had to get his family out safely before the Iraqi's returned.

Salem's cousin Bashar joined them and Mahmoud and Sausan promised to follow them the next day. They set off in convoy in the early hours of the morning towards the Saudi border in three cars. Salem, Sara, Mahmoud and his mother in my car, Jamal, Khawla, Naif and grandmother in another car and Bashar in his car.

The Iraqi's had turned the last fire station, before the border, into their final check point and around five thirty in the morning Salem's convoy joined the long queues of cars waiting to be interviewed and given a permit allowing them to leave the country. As they waited Salem and

Jamal checked the faces of those driving past in army cars, afraid that their names might already be on their way to the final check point and they would be captured again.

They had left in such a hurry that they had very limited supplies of food and water but the other Kuwaitis in the queue happily kept them supplied with sustenance.

Eventually around 2pm they reached the check point and the heads of each family were called in to be questioned. Salem and Sara went together and handed over their passports and Civil I.D.'s. They were asked where they lived, what they had left behind and if there was anyone remaining in the house. To get permission to leave they had to sign a paper stating that they held no claim to anything in Kuwait. It felt humiliating having to talk to your enemy in such a way, being so polite to them in order to get yourself and family to a place of safety. For Salem it felt at if he was signing away his identity, his nationality, as if his very existence was being stripped from him. As the formalities were finished, Salem stood alone and wept, he felt empty inside. He had just given up everything that made him feel proud to be a Kuwaiti.

As they headed towards the border there was no going back and the tears began to flow for everyone. They would be safe at last, but when would they return to Kuwait and what would they be returning to. Would they ever again see the family that they had left behind?

At the Saudi border they had to have their identity verified by the Kuwaiti and Saudi Committees set up to process the hoards of people arriving, before being allowed into the country. In their haste to leave they had had no time to make photocopies of their passports as other families had. Fortunately Salem was immediately recognized by a colleague of Marwan who managed to process their papers for them quickly, getting their documents approved and stamped by both the Kuwait and Saudi authorities without the long wait that most families had to endure. They were then given some accommodation in a school building and were shown around the facilities by one of the committee. Salem went back to the office with them where they let him make that oh so important phone call to me.

The next day they waited for Mahmoud and Sausan to arrive. Salem met them at the border and saw them safely through. They stayed another night at the school and then set off for Riyadh where they registered at the Kuwaiti Embassy and were sent to stay in a hotel, courtesy of the government. The Embassy told Salem that Marwan was working in Oman, at the Kuwaiti Embassy and after Salem spoke to him Marwan travelled to Riyadh to reunite with them. About a week after they left, Faisal arrived. He told them that the day after they had gone to Saudi Arabia the Iraqis came to the house looking for them again. Granddad told them that they had left the country so after a thorough search of the house they then went up to Uncles place. The soldiers moved into the house with the family for three days, waiting to see if Salem would return. Two of Uncles sons managed to escape and went to warn Faisal to keep away from his father's house. Uncle's family had been taking care of some police dogs which had been released from the police college at the beginning of the invasion. The soldiers shot them all. On the fourth day they took Uncle, Nawal and Uncles eldest daughter to the capital governorate, which was used as a place of interrogation and from which we had heard terrible tales of torture. At this point Faisal decided to leave and we heard no more news of them until after Liberation.

They spent a week in Riyadh getting new passports and as Marwan needed a car, he and Salem drove my car to Muscat, where it stayed until liberation. Salem returned to the family and they set off for Jeddah, where they managed to locate Salem's father. They had lots of relatives there who were very welcoming and offered them everything they needed from accommodation to cars. Wherever they went the Saudi people were extremely kind and generous and did everything they could to help their refugee neighbours. Salem got everyone settled and then went to the Embassy to see how he could get himself to England.

By the end of December Salem was back with me, safe and sound, and on 2nd January we went to London for the Free Kuwait March from the Kuwaiti Embassy to Hyde Park. Someone had smuggled out of Kuwait horrific pictures of dead and tortured Kuwaitis which had been made into placards. These surely would bring the message home to those still unsure of whether a war was justified to save those souls still in Kuwait and suffering at the hands of the Iraqis. Thousands of people were in Hyde Park listening to some very emotional speeches and as we started to make our way home I was handed an anti-war leaflet. I am normally a very peace-loving person who doesn't like to cause a scene, but I just couldn't handle this. I turned on the woman and started yelling at her that if someone didn't do something about Saddam Hussein soon then he would be sending nuclear bombs her way before long, and the only thing that Saddam Hussein understood was war. Negotiation would not stop him. Salem took my arm and calmed me down. I think he was as surprised by my outburst as I was!

On the 16th January, while staying at Simon and Jane's in Stevenage the Liberation of Kuwait began. Simon and Jane had gone to bed and Salem and I stayed up watching the news, as usual, when suddenly there was a newsflash saying that the air attack had started and the liberation of Kuwait had begun. Our cheers must have woken the whole street! At last, something was happening. Simon and Jane got up for a celebratory drink with us and as we sat glued to the television my euphoria sank as I thought about Granddad and Heather and Yousef. Would the bombs meant for Iraqi troops also be landing on them? I prayed for their safety and that it would all be over soon.

We spent many anxious hours watching the different news reports and as Liberation was finally declared on 26th February, six weeks after the Gulf War began, we sat in amazement and joy, and not without some envy, as the Kuwaitis emerged from their houses waving the national flag that had been forbidden for the last seven months, and greeted the victorious allied troops as they made their way into Kuwait.

We scanned the footage, recording it in the process, hoping to see someone we knew. Heather told me later that the first time they ventured out of the house after the war she was horrified to come across a camera crew as they had no electricity or water and she hadn't been able to wash her hair!

RETURN TO KUWAIT

We were itching to get back to Kuwait, but as the oil fires raged and there was still no electricity or water, wondered how long it would be before we would be allowed back in. Marwan had now moved to Dammam, in Saudi Arabia, close to the Kuwaiti border and was involved in providing permits allowing residents to return. He managed to get back into Kuwait briefly and reported back to us that Granddad was fit and well and very proud to have kept the house and cars secure.

Salem flew back to Jeddah and then with one of his step-brothers drove to Dammam to see Marwan. Salem wanted to carry on that night into Kuwait but Marwan persuaded them to rest a while and they set off the next morning. Salem was taking some goodies back to Heather for me, amongst them chocolate and hairspray! I knew these would be appreciated and would raise a smile! The skies were black with smoke from the oil fires and there was damage and destruction everywhere. They went straight to the house in Andalus and saw Granddad sitting by the door having his breakfast. He was so pleased to see them and told them of how he had sent the Iraqi's away when they tried to steal the cars and loot the house on their desperate flight from Kuwait. He described the amazing feeling of the day of Liberation and how he took water and food to the American soldiers and invited them in to the house for refreshments. I'm sure they loved his colourful language!

As the days passed the rest of the family slowly began to return. Our telephone was one of the few that had an international line operating so I managed to keep in touch with them all without too much trouble.

Salems Uncle, his daughter and Nawal had been taken to Basra and when the uprising in the South happened they escaped with many others and made the long walk back to Kuwait. All of them had suffered terrible torture during their incarceration. Uncle often talked about it which I think helped, but the girls found it much more difficult.

My employers, Sally and Ken, had given Salem a key to their house in Andalus to go and see what kind of state it was in. They lived a few blocks away and we had been there several times in happier days. Salem immediately saw that the house had been set on fire but still managed to get inside. It was completely dark as there was still no electricity and he stumbled into the lounge area. He took out his lighter and as he lit it jumped back, startled as he saw a charred skeleton in front of him balanced between two chairs. He went to report it to the police station and on further investigation discovered from the neighbours that the house was used by Iraqi intelligence. We never did find out who that poor soul was. I then had the unenviable task of telling Sally and Ken the whole story and that nothing much remained of their home and belongings.

I had the opportunity to start a temporary job in England working for a canal boat company for the summer season and after discussing it with Salem decided to take it, as he didn't think I would be able to do much in Kuwait for a few months to come.

Salem had been asked to go and manage the office of the new Minister of Housing, a job he thoroughly enjoyed, and he was lucky enough to be part of a delegation that came to London in June. He was able to come and spend a couple of days with us at Simon and Jane's house before going back to Kuwait, which was great as it coincided with my birthday. He also raised a few eyebrows when the taxi came to collect him dressed in full national dress!

Heather and Yousef also came back to England for a visit and came to stay at my parents for a few days. It was fantastic to see them, we reminisced a lot and I got to hear what life was like during the war and how the sound of the bombs falling over Kuwait was so loud it blew all the doors open.

It was a year after I had left Kuwait that I finally returned. It was very emotional and my eyes filled with tears as the plane touched down on Kuwaiti soil. I was so grateful that all our friends and family had survived and that our home was still in one piece. Salem drove me around the country showing me now famous landmarks of destruction. All along the sea front trenches had been dug and you could still read the calculations scribbled on the walls describing the missile launcher bearings. Every building along the sea front had a circle painted on it, some in different colours. Apparently this showed which Iraqi unit each building was controlled by. Some buildings were completely destroyed, some during the war, others set on fire by the Iraqis, trying to destroy as much as possible before they hurriedly left the country.

We went to the "Valley of Death". The road that I had travelled on as I left towards Iraq, just as you reach Mutla ridge. For as far as you could see the road was scattered with burnt out vehicles and trucks loaded with looted goods. The allies had bombed them as the road became jammed with traffic trying to escape the country. It must have been horrific. The bodies had been removed but there still remained discarded articles of clothing and shoes strewn all over the place. It was a horrible sight.

In the area of Qurain there is a house where eighteen members of the Kuwaiti resistance made a last valiant stand against the Iraqi military might, just a few days before the liberation. The Iraqis blasted the building with tanks and heavy artillery, causing massive destruction and killing eleven of those brave souls. The house has been left exactly as it was found after liberation, an eerie tribute to those who lost their lives amidst an otherwise untouched urban maze. It would later be turned into a museum of sorts and was visited by Norman Shwarzkopf, who left a few words saluting the bravery of those men who lost their lives.

Thousands of mines had been planted all over the country and there was also a lot of unexploded ordnance around. The clearing continued everywhere and some areas were still out of bounds as they hadn't been covered yet. Every few days there was a massive explosion as the army detonated all the unexploded bombs that they had cleared.

The last of the oil fires was extinguished not long after I returned but the evidence of them could still be seen. Black specks were all over the windows and the dust that settled daily was black and oily. Salem's white clothes were covered in small black specks too.

I went to my place of work. The entrance had been bricked up but the Iraqi's had still managed to get in. They had broken into the safe and company documents had been strewn everywhere. Although there were two bathrooms in the building the Iraqis had chosen to use the floor to defecate on. As the staff went to inspect the many apartments that we provided rented furniture to, they discovered that this was a very common practice! I was soon back at work and trying to get the hundreds of pieces of paper into some kind of order again! Surprisingly, after days of sorting, very little was actually missing.

Life gradually began to get back to normal. Kuwait began to boom as the reconstruction began. Some friends came back to Kuwait others never returned. There were over six hundred missing prisoners of war that could not be located and Saddam Hussein claimed he had no knowledge of. Over six hundred families awoke each day hoping to hear some news of their loved ones. For most it would take eleven years to discover their fate.

It wasn't long before we carried on with our lives as if nothing had ever happened. But, always in the back of my mind was the fact that, even after all this, Saddam Hussein was still in power in Iraq and that it was only a matter of time before we would hear his drums of war pounding again.

You may wonder what happened to the people in my story......

Sadly Salem's father and both grandparents have passed away and we eventually sold the house in Andalus and moved to another area closer to Kuwait City.

Sara had a baby girl who was born shortly after the Liberation while they were still in Saudi Arabia.

Salem's mother is now proud to have a British daughter-in-law coming from one of the countries that came to liberate Kuwait! Long may it last!

Uncle and his family still live in the same house in Andalus.

Yousef's mother passed away and Heather and Yousef have now built their own house and have four lovely children. Yousef who is an avid diver played a big part in raising the boats sunk by the Iraqi forces. Their own boat, on which we had many happy trips out to the coral reefs at Kubar Island, was ransacked and severely damaged by the Iraqis.

Pat and Alex never returned to Kuwait and made their home in Cyprus.

Cathy and Alec now live in Australia and have twins that were conceived whilst "Guests" of

Saddam Hussein, somewhere in Iraq!

AUTHORS NOTE

My story is one of many. There are those who were not as lucky as we were and suffered terribly at the hands of the Iraqis. The memories of the invasion will stay with us always and for many the memories are so painful that they will have a profound affect on the rest of their lives. The courage and kindness of the Kuwaitis, who risked their lives to hide, protect and feed the westerners trapped in their country should not be forgotten.

I dedicate this book to those who lost their lives and loved ones during the invasion and liberation and to those who had to wait eleven long years to discover the fate of their missing family members who were Prisoners of War. I hope this recent history is kept alive for coming generations to learn from and I hope that Saddam Hussein's capture and punishment will give retribution and peace to all those millions of lives that he affected.

Life has changed a lot for us since the invasion. We now spend a lot of time in Lebanon......but that's another story.

ISBN 1412099954-4